LE.
DIS/

MW01234302

IN A
NUTSHELL

A Parent-Teacher Manual for Understanding and the
Management of Dyslexia, Dysgraphia, Dyscalculia and Dyspraxia

by

Dr Swaroop Rawal

HEALTH HARMONY

An imprint of
B. Jain Publishers (P) Ltd.
An ISO 9001 : 2000 Certified Company
USA — Europe — India

LEARNING DISABILITIES IN A NUTSHELL

First Edition: 2010
1st Impression: 2010

Published by Kuldeep Jain for

HEALTH ❁ HARMONY
An imprint of
B. JAIN PUBLISHERS (P) LTD.
An ISO 9001 : 2000 Certified Company
1921/10, Chuna Mandi, Paharganj, New Delhi 110 055 (INDIA)
Tel.: +91-11-4567 1000 • Fax: +91-11-4567 1010
Email: info@bjain.com • Website: www.bjainbooks.com

Printed in India
J.J. Offset Printers

ISBN: 978-81-319-0665-1

A person with a learning disability may experience a cycle of academic failures and lowered self esteem. Having this handicap, or living with someone who has it can bring crushing frustration. Our children can be successful in school environments that support their special learning needs and as parents /teachers we must ensure they get the help they deserve in regular schools.

It is important to remember that a person with a learning disability can learn. The disability usually only affects certain limited areas of a child's development. In fact, rarely are learning disabilities severe enough to impair a person's potential to live a happy life.

Above all, I believe the greatest joy that we can experience is to see a smile on the faces of our children. So no matter what issues and problems our children face, we should try and be understanding, caring and loving, as opposed to being aggressive, judgemental and pushy. That one smile on your child's face is worth a million PhDs.

Security, trust/faith, self respect/dignityand love are the four most important requirements that our children have from us. These are the four pillars on which we should build our relationship with our children.

So read on, make use of all the information that has been so studiously collected, and importantly, start collecting your million PhDs.

Aamir Khan

FOREWORD

Well, first of all I must confess that I am not an academic [
nor am I an expert on learning disabilities and difficulties. S
frankly, I was most hesitant to write this foreword (whic
explains why I took so long, Swaroop). However, I do und
the need to make a book like this reach out to a larger num
people so I guess that's where I come in.

Well, here it goes.

Let me start by congratulating Swaroop for coming o
such a well-researched and comprehensive book on the
learning issues that children can face. It is clear and simply
whichis quite a relief.

It is most important for all those of us who plan to e
teaching profession to read and understand a book of th
Also for parents and potential parents, as it goes a long
helping us understand the issues our children might face.

All of us have strengths and weaknesses.

As adults, we need to help our children recognise
their strengths and more importantly, we need to und
their weaknesses so that we are able to help them deal wi
better.

The major barrier in the way of competent schoo
children with learning disabilities is not only the preser
learning disability, but also the lack of understanding
disability and the difficulties it causes. This book is us
parents/teachers who have to grapple with problems f
children with learning disabilities and the problems whi
perplex them.

PREFACE

I have begun this book with a journal entry of a personal experience in the summer of 2002, in USA. My journey of discovery becomes lucid in the narrative seeing that it enabled me to become sensitive to the perspective of my learning disabled students. I believe that one of the most important skills for a teacher to possess is empathy. Empathic teachers are able to put themselves in the shoes of their students and perceive the world through their student's eyes. Empathic educators connect more effectively and constructively with students and thus enable effective learning. Empathic parents and siblings enhance their own emotional and social competence and in turn create a caring community.

While on tour of the play I was performing in USA, I was prepared to face a bit of tight security. The troupe had visited USA in September 2001 and had heard and read about air-travel becoming bothersome after 9/11. However, I was not prepared for what actually happened again and again at all the airports in USA.

The first flight I had to catch was to Tampa. Our team consisting of nine members reached JFK three hours before the flight so as to have plenty of time in hand seeing that we had loads of luggage consisting of our personal and theatrical baggage. When I checked my bags, the computer signalled an extra security check. I was asked to stand aside, while the lady at the checking in counter asked an assistant to take my luggage, my ticket and boarding pass. I was politely but very firmly asked not to even touch my bags! On my part, I was not the least bit concerned and followed the assistant to the X-ray machine. Obviously, my belongings passed the inspection. I was given my boarding pass and asked to proceed to the flight.

When the flight was announced, we walked towards the aeroplane with the other passengers. At the gate, I was asked to go in for another check. The security staff went through everything in my hand luggage, she flicked through my books, opened my lipsticks, my purse, everything, I really felt violated. The worst was the humiliating body-check. I was asked to take off my jacket, belt and even my shoes. I could feel everybody's eyes on me as they walked past me into the flight.

This pattern was repeated for the next six flights. I started dreading checking-in. Trying to rationalise the act, I looked for signs, I compared boarding tickets with the rest of the troupe to see if I could decipher their code, which sent me to the extra check. Why did my ticket show up on the computer while the rest of the team didn't have a problem?

It was always my name that was picked up. I started feeling like someone who was being tried for a crime she had not committed. I could feel every one's eyes on me, as I stood there, red in the face, seething with anger, nails marking my palm. I had done nothing wrong.

Before every flight I started feeling tense and grouchy. My eyes would go all swimmy. After all the 'checking' I would sit on the flight exhausted, belt up, close my eyes and sleep, as I tried to shut myself to the outside world.

It was after the eighth or ninth flight that my thoughts went to my students with a learning disability and I began to feel like they probably did being treated unfairly and sometimes even unkindly I began to understand how they must have felt when, for no fault of theirs they were picked upon in class. I began to understand how children felt when they were labelled 'lazy' and a 'shirker' when they actually had something amiss in the way they processed information. I put myself in their place, and my feelings began to suggest their feelings and the reason for their behavior. From an interested observer I changed into an 'insider'.

Empathy is when somebody has a similar emotional state as another as a result of perceiving that person's situation. I knew I began to empathize with my students.

Understanding is a very personal thing. 'Only connect...' is Forster's epigraph for *Howard's End*.

Journal: Summer 2002

The aim of this book is to help bridge the gap between research and practice in the field of learning disability. It is written for all the learning disabled children, their teachers, parents and siblings because I believe that learning disability is not a burden. If we can empathise with and understand the differences in the children with learning disability, we will help them to overcome adversity and become resilient to learn how to face the problems they have to deal with in their young world, to empower them so they can grow into well adjusted adults. We will enable the learning disabled child to deal effectively with the demands and challenges of everyday life and find their own place in the world.

Dr Swaroop Rawal

ACKNOWLEDGEMENTS

There are a number of people who have played an important role in the process and creation of this book. I would like to express my sincere appreciation for them.

Dr Madhuri Kulkarni and Dr Sunil Karande without whose help, advice and encouragement I would have not been able to complete my study. I do realize that appreciation for their guidance cannot be expressed in merely a few words.

Dr Smita Desai for introducing me to 'Learning Disability' and for the encouragement she gave me during my early years in teaching. The inspiration she gave enabled me to reflect and transform my practice.

I would also like to express my genuine appreciation for my family for their unending support.

Last but not the least, I would like to express my immense gratitude to all my teachers who taught from their heart and enthused me to continue learning and to grow.

PUBLISHER'S NOTE

Dr Swaroop Rawal's book on 'Learning Disabilities in a Nutshell' comes at a time when there is a growing need for quality education standards. It is a scholarly work but never too obscure for parents with children who have learning disability problems. It has been written with compassion and sensitivity and cannot be anything but encouraging to all concerned. Dyslexia and related learning disabilities, Dr Rawal points out, are not a disease. Therefore, they cannot be 'cured'. What is important is to recognize that there is a problem and to react to it in time. There may be associated emotional problems too in which case proper counselling can certainly save a child's self-esteem and self-worth and make him a useful member of the society.

Let us, with Dr Rawal's clarion call rise to the occasion, realizing that every schoolchild is equally important, whether he is a bright child or a slow learner. Let us do all we can on a war footing, to meet the nation's hunger for quality education so that today's children can grow up into caring, responsible and useful adults tomorrow.

Kuldeep Jain
C.E.O., B. Jain Publishers (P) Ltd.

ONE DAY IN THE CLASSROOM

I sat in the classroom,
trying
trying
trying hard to read well.
The words were whirling
pitching like a slight leaf on turbulent water,
it feels like when you put your hands in water to catch some dirt
you think you have caught it
but it slips away between your fingers.

The tree I see outside the school window
is alive with shining eyes and winged creatures.
A pigeon flies in, carrying a dry twig;
it falls,
he tries to pick it up
trying
trying
have another go I say.

Have another go,
why is reading soooooo difficult!
I want to read well,
but words are not my best friends.
They play hide and seek with me,
sometimes I catch them,
sometimes when I think I have caught them
but I have actually caught some word else.
Another pigeon flies in to help,
two more fly in and look on

I can count four pigeons.
They scuffle,
feathers are flying
and some dry leaves
in the breeze
up and down
in no particular direction.

In no particular direction
letters and words are printed on the page.
They are a jumbled mess.
They muddle my brain.
They are so tricky
They tire me out.
I feel as if I have run a hundred miles.

I draw the life outside in my book.
The tree is perfectly formed, the pigeons in one row.
Details of the wings,
eyes and tiny feet.
Leaves and flowers bloom on my page.
What are you doing?

What are you doing?
Let me see the book.
The sound brings me back to class
away from real life.
Sweaty hands make the pencil slip,
it falls,
I drop the book.
She picks it up and looks at me.
I am startled.

The pigeons fly away.
Will she yell?
The tree is forlorn.
Will she take out the ruler?
The breeze stops blowing.
Will she pull me up
like others before her?

'Wow!' she says.
Is that a teacher's word?
'What a beautiful drawing…
Read these lines,' she says
She knows I can't.
I struggle.
she is standing close by...
I am scared.
She points to each word one by one.
I plod on but read correctly,
Not all the words but most.

'If you draw for me
as beautifully as you can'
she whispers,
'I will teach you to read
as well as I can'.

Dr Swaroop Rawal

CONTENTS

CONTENTS

CHAPTER 1

A BRIEF HISTORY OF LEARNING DISABILITIES

1. A German physician, Franz Joseph Gall, is accredited as the first major figure to investigate the relationship between brain injury and mental impairment. Gall is known for noting the effect of brain damage on what today would be termed as Broca's aphasia.

2. Broca is generally known for being the one who did the most to promote the idea that speech functions primarily reside in the left side of the brain. Broca concluded that a small section of the left side of the brain was responsible for speech. This area which is located in the inferior left frontal lobe, has come to be called Broca's area; persons who have speech problems involving slow, laborious, dysfluent speech are said to have Broca's aphasia.

3. 1874: Wernicke a Polish physician studied brain affected patients who had fluent and unlabored speech, but the sentences spoken were often meaningless. He called this disorder sensory aphasia, which has become known as Wernicke's aphasia.

4. 1878: Dr. Kussmaul (Germany) described a man with normal intelligence but unable to read in spite of an 'adequate' education. He called this condition 'word-blindness'. Kussmaul gave birth to the idea of specific reading disability.

5. 1896: Dr. Pringle Morgan (UK) described a 14-year-old boy with reading difficulty: his eyes are normal, there is no hemianopia and his eyesight is good. The schoolmaster declared that 'he would be the smartest lad in the school if the instruction were entirely oral'(Morgan, 1896, p. 1378).

6. Hinshelwood, (1917, p. 99) introduced the earliest concept of special education as one-to-one: 'It is not possible to teach such children in ordinary elementary schools.... The first condition of successful instruction in such cases...is that the child must have personal instruction and be taught alone.'

7. 1925: Dr Samuel Orton (USA) proposed the theory of 'specific learning difficulty' and also offered the term 'strephosymbolia' from the Greek words, (strepho-twist) and (symbolon, symbol). The prefix 'strepho' has been chosen to indicate the turning or reversals. 'Symbolon' is used in its original meaning of 'word', 'sign' or 'token' (Orton, 1925). Orton was one of the first to introduce the idea of multisensory training

8. 1936: Anna Gillingham and Bessie Stillman published 'Remedial Training for Children with Specific Disability in Reading, Spelling and Penmanship'. Even today, special educators still use several of the ideas of Orton and Gillingham and Stillman or the Orton-Gillingham Approach; a phonics-based, multisensory method using the visual, auditory, and kinesthetic modalities for reading-decoding and spelling instruction.

9. 1963: Dr. Samuel Kirk (USA) first used term 'learning disabilities'.

10. 1969: 'The Children with Specific Learning Disabilities Act (USA)' passed.

11. 1977: Public law fine tuned ensuring rights of American children with SpLD to 'appropriate evaluation' and 'management' of their problem.

12. In the 1960s, a majority of the definitions of learning disabilities alluded to a neurological basis for learning disabilities. However, it was not until the 1980s and especially the 1990s that the biological basis for learning disabilities found support. It was also in the 1990s that the hereditary nature of learning disabilities was indicated.

13. 1994: The concept of inclusion and inclusive education emerged. The UNESCO's Salamanca Statement (1994) states that 'inclusion and participation are essential to human dignity and the exercise of 'human rights' and 'the fundamental principle of the inclusive school says that all children should learn together, wherever possible, regardless of any difficulties or differences they may have'.

History of Specific Learning Disability Movement in Mumbai, India

1. 1987: SNDT College Mumbai starts B.Ed. (Special Education) course: Special Educators for remediation available.

2. 1992: Parent group start 'lobbying' for recognition of SpLD so that these children continue education in regular schools. Specific learning disability (SpLD) which includes dyslexia, dysgraphia, dyscalculia is commonly referred to as 'learning disability' or 'LD' in India.

3. 1995: Maharashtra Dyslexia Association formed by parents of SpLD children.

4. 1996: L.D. clinic at LTMG (Sion) Hospital started by Prof. Madhuri Kulkarni.

5. 1996: Govt. of Maharashtra issues G.R. which grants provisions for first time in India; but for standards IX and X only.

6. 1999: ICSE and CBSE boards also grant provisions.

7. 2000: Provisions extended from standard I to XII.

8. 2003: Provisions extended to college courses; seats 'reserved' for SpLD in physically handicapped category in colleges, including professional course.

(Karande, 2007)

CHAPTER 2

WHAT ARE LEARNING DISABILITIES?

Learning disabilities have been studied for over a century in the west. The earliest case studies were described in medical journals dating back to 1891. Yet, there is a lot of ambiguity in meanings attached to learning disability and several diverse terms used to characterise learning problems. In this chapter I have tried to explain the term learning disability and the definition of it. I have explained what the definition of learning disability actually means so as to elucidate the enigma identified as learning disability. In this chapter I have also traced what the traits of learning disability are.

A learning disability is a neurological disorder. In simple terms, a learning disability results from a difference in the way a person's brain is 'wired'. Children with learning disabilities are as smart as or smarter than their peers. However, they may have trouble in reading, writing, spelling, reasoning, recalling and/or organizing information. Importantly, learning disability cannot be cured or fixed; it is a lifelong concern. Nevertheless, with the correct encouragement, support and intervention, children with learning disabilities can succeed in school and have flourishing careers later in life.

Parents can help children with learning disabilities achieve such success by encouraging their strengths, knowing their weaknesses, understanding the educational system, working with professionals and learning about strategies by dealing with specific difficulties.

Learning disability (LD) or Specific learning disability (SpLD) is a lifelong neuro-developmental disorder which manifests in childhood as persistent difficulties in learning to efficiently read (dyslexia), write (dysgraphia) or do simple mathematical calculations (dyscalculia) despite normal intelligence, conventional schooling, intact hearing and vision, adequate motivation and sociocultural opportunity.

Way back in 1963 Dr Samuel Kirk, who was deeply involved in research aimed at understanding the inconsistency seen in the special students, learning style, which is officially credited with coining the term 'learning disabilities'. He used it as a means to identify groups of what he called 'perceptually handicapped children'. This term has become the most commonly used label in special education.

The concept of learning disability (Hallahan and Cruickshank, 1973) included:

'...children who could see and hear and who do not have marked intellectual deficits, but who show deviations in behavior and in psychological development to such an extent that they are unable to adjust at home or to learn by ordinary methods in school.' (p. 4)

In the eighties, researchers and educators studied various techniques to understand the needs of students suffering from learning disability. By the late 1980's a copious number of theories were produced and were slowly and steadily being established and concurred (Hallahan and Mercer, 2001). By the turn of the twenty-first century it was established that students were capable of learning task-appropriate strategies that facilitated academic success. Many studies confirmed earlier conclusions that learning disability may be the result of neurological dysfunction and that heredity is linked to the varying learning disabilities.

Attitudes and understanding of learning disabilities have changed dramatically over the past few decades. Previously many educators believed there was no such thing as a learning disability, that the child was either lazy or just plain stupid. No educator would subscribe to that concept today. However, sadly many learning disabled children still see themselves in that light (Sharma, 2004).

It is now known that a learning disability is not connected to mental retardation; the learning disabled frequently have high IQs. It is also not a single disorder, but includes disabilities in any of areas related to reading, language and mathematics. These include different forms of reading-learning disability like dyslexia, in addition to dyscalculia for mathematics and short term memory disorders.

During the past few decades, the understanding of learning disability has changed radically. However, it is a tremendous challenge to identify and diagnose and assist children with learning disability as the concept is still new in many developing countries (Ramaa, 2000). Research conducted in learning disability in India has been primarily done over the last two decades (Ramaa, 2000) and is today comparable with the research carried out in the west nearly half a century ago (Karnath, 2001). India is thought to have approximately ninety million people with varying degrees of learning disabilities and an average class in schools has about five students with learning disabilities (Sunil Thomas, Bhanutej and John, 2003). Yet we do not have a clear idea about the incidence and prevalence of learning disabilities in India (Karnath, 2001).

It is extremely important for parents and children to understand about learning disability as stumbling blocks such as lack of awareness, indifference and apathy can hamper success.

The term 'learning disability' is used in USA to refer to problems similar to those described in the UK as 'Specific learning difficulty'. There are several definitions of SpLD, LD and dyslexia drawn on in the UK, the USA and other countries. The definition issued by the National Joint Committee for Learning Disabilities (NJCLD, 1981) is the definition schools and Special Educators in India refer to:

'Learning disability is a general term that refers to a heterogeneous group of disorders manifested by significant difficulties in acquisition and use of listening, speaking, reading, writing, reasoning, or mathematical abilities. These disorders are intrinsic to the individual, presumed to be due to central nervous dysfunction, and may occur across a life span. Problems in self-regulatory behaviors, social perception and social interaction may exist with learning disabilities but do not by themselves constitute a learning disability. Although learning disabilities may occur concomitantly with other handicapping conditions (for example, sensory impairment, mental retardation, serious emotional disturbance) or with extrinsic influences (such as cultural differences, insufficient or inappropriate instruction), they are not the result of those conditions or influences.'(p.1)

The NJCLD Revised Definition (1988)

The NJCLD revised definition was in response to the Learning Disabilities Association of America (LDA) definition's emphasis on the lifelong nature of learning disabilities and the Interagency Committee on Learning Disabilities (ICLD) listing of social skills deficits as a type of learning disability. The NJCLD revised definition agreed with the former but disagreed with the latter.

Learning disabilities is a general term that refers to a heterogeneous group of disorders manifested by significant difficulties in the acquisition and use of listening, speaking, reading, writing, reasoning, or mathematical abilities. These disorders are intrinsic to the individual, presumed to be due to central nervous system dysfunction, and may occur across the life span. Problems of self-regulatory behaviors, social perception, and social interaction may exist with learning disabilities but do not by themselves constitute a learning disability. Although learning disabilities may occur concomitantly with other handicapping conditions (for example, sensory impairment, mental retardation, serious emotional disturbance) or with extrinsic influences (such as cultural differences, insufficient or inappropriate instruction), they are not the result of those conditions or influences. (NJCLD, 1988, p. 1)

Individuals with Disabilities Education Act (IDEA) Reauthorized definition (1997). The definition in federal law has remained virtually unchanged since the one included in P.L. 94-142:

1. In General—The term 'specific learning disability' means a disorder in one or more of the basic psychological processes involved in understanding or in using language, spoken or written, which may manifest itself in imperfect ability to listen, think, speak, read, write, spell, or do mathematical calculations.
2. Disorders Included—conditions as perceptual disabilities, brain injury, minimal brain dysfunction, dyslexia, and developmental aphasia.
3. Disorders Not Included—such term does not include a learning problem that is primarily the result of visual, hearing, or motor disabilities, of mental retardation, of emotional disturbance, or of environmental, cultural, or economic disadvantage. (IDEA Amendments of 1997, Sec. 602(26), p. 13).

What does this definition mean?

Surprisingly, there is no clear and widely accepted definition of 'learning disabilities'. Additionally, several diverse terms are used, such as learning difficulty, specific learning difficulty, dyslexia, specific learning dyslexia, specific reading retardation, learning disability, specific learning disability, and special educational needs. This makes it extremely confusing for layman, parents and teachers. For the reason of the multidisciplinary nature of the field, there is ongoing debate on the issue of definition, and there are currently at least 12 definitions that appear in the professional literature. However, these contrasting definitions (including the above stated definition) do agree on certain factors:

1. The learning disabled have difficulties with academic achievement and progress. Discrepancies exist between a person's potential for learning and what he actually learns.
2. The learning disabled show an uneven pattern of development (language development, physical development, academic development and/or perceptual development).
3. Learning problems are not due to environmental disadvantage.
4. Learning problems are not due to mental retardation or emotional disturbance.

This means that learning disability interferes with the learning process.

Inclusion clause – includes neurological problems which may or may not be severe but we see in a small percentage. It infers that learning problems in the child are of neurological nature that has to do with the nervous system.

The basic psychological process means that the facility or ability to:

1. Receive information

2. To understand
3. To express and interpret

It has to do with the working of the brain.

Language based –understanding and using a language. A child with a learning disability is as able as any other child, except in one or two areas of their learning. For instance, they may find it difficult to recognise letters, or to cope with numbers or reading.

The three key factors which are highlighted in this definition are:

1. The child with learning disability shows a discrepancy between intelligence and achievement. A child with learning disability has average to above average intelligence quotient (IQ).
2. Mental retardation, visual and hearing impairment and emotional and or behavioral disorder must be ruled out.
3. Learning disability is a psychological processing disorder and assumes a central nervous dysfunction.

A Discrepancy between Intelligence and Achievement

Importantly, learning disability is related to the learning process of the child. It is an impediment only if there is a problem in achievability. There has to be occurrence of low achievability that is hindering performance and results in school. All underachievers may not necessarily have learning disability. This is because a child with learning disability has a neurological deficit whereas an underachiever may have an environmental problem or an emotional disturbance which is affecting his grades. A discrepancy between intelligence and achievement indicates that the child is not attaining grades or marks as much as he is intelligently capable of. This means that there is a discrepancy between observed and expected achievements. The expected achievement is based on the child's IQ. The observed achievements are not as much as other children of her chronological age. One or two years below the expected level of achievements is the most prevalent reference point for assessing the discrepancy.

Thus a child has a learning disability if:

He has a significantly greater difficulty in learning than the majority of children of his age.

His grades are one or two levels below the grades of children of his age.

No standard deviation or criterion range is set for students younger than 2nd standard due to problems in accessing and utilizing appropriate standard score measurements with this age group. For students younger than 2nd standard, identification of a significant discrepancy may be made through clinical judgment by the multidisciplinary team. Such students must meet all other components of the other eligibility criteria.

Vetoing Other Handicaps

Many learning disabilities are consequences of disadvantaged environments, emotional problems and poor intelligence development. Moreover, it is difficult to exclude the role played by socio-economic factors in a child's life. Nevertheless, the exclusion clause states that a child may not be identified as having a learning disability if the severe discrepancy between ability and achievement is primarily the result of:

1.   Lack of appropriate instruction in reading and math
2.   Limited English proficiency
3.   Visual Impairment
4.   Hearing Impairment
5.   Orthopedic Impairment

6. Mental Retardation
7. Emotional Disturbance
8. Environmental, economic or cultural factors
9. Motivational factors, and
10. Situational trauma

Central Nervous System Dysfunction

A neuropsychiatrist Alfred Strauss, created the diagnostic category of minimal brain damage in children. He presumed that children with learning disability, who were not mentally retarded, hearing impaired, or emotionally disturbed, had minimal brain damage (Duchan, 2001). His work met with disapproval in the research community. Regardless of the inability of researchers to prove learning disability was caused by neurological dysfunction, parents welcomed the explanation of why their child was not performing well in school.

The NJCLD asserts that the idea of central nervous system dysfunction as a basis for learning disabilities is appropriate. This must not, however, restrict the identification of a learning disability to the physician. In fact, many individuals with central nervous system dysfunction, such as individuals with cerebral palsy, do not necessarily show evidence of learning disorders. For the individual with learning disabilities, evidence of central nervous system dysfunction may or may not be elicited during the course of a medical-neurological examination. The critical elements in the diagnosis of learning disabilities are elicited during psychological, educational and/or language assessments. This suggests that the significant discrepancy and processing deficits are presumed to be intrinsic to the student and due to central nervous system dysfunction. However, medical confirmation of a central nervous system dysfunction is not required for the student to meet the eligibility criteria.

What are the Traits of Learning Disabilities?

Some features of a learning disabled child are:

- Looks typical but does not learn typically
- Is intelligent and sometimes is also gifted
- Has reading, writing and /or maths achievement that are significantly below child's capacity level
- Tight, awkward pencil grip and body position
- Illegible handwriting
- Avoiding writing or drawing tasks
- Tiring quickly while writing
- Saying words out loud while writing
- Unfinished or omitted words in sentences
- Difficulty organizing thoughts on paper
- Difficulty with syntax structure and grammar
- Large gap between written ideas and understanding demonstrated through speech
- May have a short attention span
- Has poor listening skills
- Has trouble following instructions
- Has trouble following directions
- Does not seem to be trying, acts lazy and /or is defiant
- Confuses left and right
- Sometimes is awkward, clumsy and uses immature movements
- Shows poor motor co-ordination
- Shows evidence of immature behavior
- Has difficulty with tasks employing paper and pencil
- Produces reversals (mixes up 'b' and 'd') and rotations ('b instead of 'p') in written work
- Displays general disorganisation, poor organisation of time and space
- Is inconsistent in behavior and work

- Frequently displays exceptional ability in sports, arts, science and verbalisation

With reference to more specific reading and writing errors throughout the junior years in school, some of the early indicators of learning disability that can be spotted by parents and teachers are:

- Has difficulty fastening buttons and shoelaces
- Shoes are often worn on the wrong foot
- Appears clumsy and accident prone
- Has difficulty in skipping, hopping or clapping a simple rhythm
- Has difficulty in catching, throwing or kicking a ball
- Has difficulty in carrying out more than one instruction
- Confuses between left and right
- Has difficulty in understanding prepositions concerned with directions such as in, out, up, down, under, over, forward, backward
- Has a history of slow speech development
- Undetermined hand preference
- Poor handwriting
- Difficulty in remembering anything in sequential order, for example days of the week, months of the years, and tables
- Has difficulty in learning to tell the time. Unsure about tomorrow and yesterday
- Has difficulty in pronouncing multi-syllabic words- hopsital for hospital
- Excessive tiredness due to amount of effort and concentration required for very little result

Additionally, the commonly related symptoms of learning disabilities are:

- Poor performance on group tests

- Difficulty in discriminating size, shape and color
- Difficulty with temporal (time) concepts
- Distorted concept of body image
- Reversals in writing and reading
- General awkwardness
- Poor visual-motor coordination
- Slowness in completing work
- Poor organizational skills
- Easily confused by instructions
- Difficulty with abstract reasoning and/or problem solving
- Disorganized thinking
- Poor short-term or long-term memory
- Impulsive behavior. No reflection on consequence of action
- Low tolerance for frustration
- Poor peer relationships
- Poor social judgment
- Lags in developmental milestones (e.g. motor, language)
- Behavior often inappropriate for situation
- Excessive variation in mood and responsiveness
- Poor adjustment to environmental changes
- Overly distractible; difficulty concentrating
- Difficulty making decisions

When considering these signs, it is essential to remember the following:

1. No one will have all these symptoms.
2. Some symptoms are more common than others.
3. All people have at least two or three of these problems to some degree.
4. The number of symptoms seen in a particular child does not give an indication as whether the disability is mild or severe. It is important to consider if the behaviors are persistent and appear in clusters.

What is not Learning Disability

1. Slow learners (IQ 71 to 84).
2. Mental retardation (IQ ≤ 70).
3. Visual handicap (>40% disability).
4. Hearing handicap (>40% disability).
5. Physical handicap (e.g. cerebral palsy).
6. Language barrier.
7. Emotional problems / Chronic medical problems.
8. Psychiatric disorders (e.g. depression) (Karande , 2008).

CHAPTER 3

ETIOLOGY OF LEARNING DISABILITIES

In this chapter I have discussed what are the causes of learning disability. Anxious parents at all times want to know what are the causes or the etiology of learning disability. There is plenty of research literature available on the etiology of it. Mostly, such literatures are extremely difficult for the normal parent to acquire and further to understand. Besides, as parents they always feel that if they know what the causes are they can be prevented. Sadly, it is difficult to associate a single factor or a group of factors to learning disability as the etiology of learning disability is extremely complex. Moreover, the parents' queries cannot be answered with certainty because research yields conflicting results or does not elucidate everything. Nevertheless, in this chapter I have attempted to give an explanation as to what causes the symptoms of learning disability.

Karande and co-researchers (2007) suggest that almost 10% of school-going children have learning disability in the form of dyslexia, dysgraphia and/ or dyscalculia. Additionally, Attention-deficit hyperactivity disorder (ADHD) occurs as a co-morbidity in about 20% of these children. Learning disability does imply a lifelong condition and, in this sense, a distinction does need to be made with those special educational needs that arise from difficulties that may be temporary (e.g. some behavioral or emotional problems). Nevertheless, learning disability is a broad term that covers a wide range of needs and problems, including dyslexia and behavioral problems and the full range of ability. A child who has such a learning disability is also defined as being a child with special educational needs. He has a disability which either prevents or hinders him from making use of educational facilities of a kind generally provided for children of his age in schools

When our children have a problem, we want to know what happened. What went wrong? What caused the problem? Is there a cure? One of the first questions parents ask when they learn their child has a learning disability is ...Why? What went wrong? Nevertheless, the causes of learning disability are complex and difficult to pin point.

There is no one single cohesive theory that explains the etiology of dyslexia. Recent functional MRI (magnetic resonance imaging) brain studies indicate that the disorder may be caused by specific deficits in the left frontotemporal region or atypical asymmetries in the left perisylvian regions (Demonet, Taylor and Chaix, 2004). What the research has again and again pointed out is that differences in the structure of the brain, as well as differences in the function of the brain, have been identified in individuals with learning disabilities. Furthermore, there is a genetic constituent or aspect, particularly with reading disabilities, that are in part hereditary. Learning disabilities are neurobiological in nature.

A single neurological problem caused learning disability; that was what the researchers and scientists believed. New evidence seems to show that the causes are more diverse and complex and that most learning disabilities do not stem from a single, specific area of the brain, but from difficulties in bringing together information from various brain regions. Today, a leading theory is that learning disabilities stem from subtle disturbances in the structure and function of the brain. Some scientists believe that, in many cases, the disturbance begins before birth. Certain biological, genetic, or environmental factors are linked with learning disabilities. The following factors may contribute to the cause of learning disability:

1. Genetics
2. Injury to the foetus
3. Medical problems the mother had during pregnancy
4. Prenatal exposure to drugs, alcohol, nicotine, or other toxic substances
5. Lead poisoning
6. Premature birth, low birth weight, or birth trauma
7. Head injury
8. Poor nutrition, either the child's or the mother's when she was pregnant

Genetic Factors

Research in the nineties pointed to the hereditary characteristic of learning disabilities. This established the fact that there may be a genetic link to learning disabilities, and that it tends to run in families. Those children with reading problems, such as hearing the separate sounds of words, are likely to have a parent with a related problem. However, it was also found that it seems doubtful that specific learning disorders are inherited directly, seeing that sometimes a parent's learning disability may be slightly different from the child's learning disability. A parent who has a writing disorder may have a child with an expressive language disorder.

Research done by Shalev and co-researchers (2001) conclude that dyscalculia, like other learning disabilities, has a significant familial aggregation, suggesting a role for genetics in the evolution of this disorder. Possibly, what is inherited is a subtle brain dysfunction that can in turn lead to a learning disability. The most likely explanation concerning genetics is that various genes are the possible causes of dyslexia. Most likely a number of genes interact to cause dyslexia rather than one specific gene.

Additionally, there may be an alternative explanation for why learning disability might seem to run in families. Some learning disabilities may actually stem from the family environment. For example, parents who have expressive language disorders might talk less to their children or the language they use may be distorted. In such cases, the child lacks a good model for acquiring language and therefore, may seem to be learning disabled.

Errors in Foetal Brain Development

Some experts think that learning disabilities can be traced to brain development, both before and after birth. Throughout pregnancy, the foetal brain develops from a few all-purpose cells into a complex organ made of billions of specialized, interconnected nerve cells called neurons. During the foetal process, brain development which is complex, things can go wrong that may alter how the neurons form or interconnect. Brain development is vulnerable to disruptions. Throughout the prenatal and postnatal periods and the first three years which are critical in brain development.

In the initial period of development the brain reproduces and creates as many as 250,000 cells per minute. There are approximately 100 billion neurons (brain cells) and about one trillion supportive cells. These cells must travel to different locations throughout the brain as it is being wired. There are trillions of connections linking the neurons from one part of the brain to the other (Fierdorowicz, 2005). If there is something in the environment that impedes the development, then changes in structure and function can occur.

Researchers suggest that during early brain development, the brain is more sensitive to trauma and toxins. Early development and later cognitive and behavioral development can be disturbed. Low birth weight, oxygen deprivation, prenatal delivery, early oxygen dependence, prenatal seizures, hemorrhages, alcohol, cigarettes, lead, cadmium, iron, chloride deficiencies, and nutritional deficiencies can all have a negative effect on brain development.

Other Factors that Affect Brain Development

In recent years the role of cerebellum has attracted the interests of neurologists. During the last thirty years research has been confirming a relationship between learning problems and poor balance and coordination. The cerebellum is the area of the brain that controls coordination and balance. It also plays a role in memory, another problem area for learning disability. The difference between a normal cerebellum and a dyslexic's cerebellum may be just a question of size. The clumsiness and poor coordination in a learning disability is very similar to the way a small child moves. It may be that the cerebellum has failed to grow with the rest of the body and is underdeveloped.

Young children who receive head injuries may also be at risk of developing learning disabilities.

Tobacco, Alcohol and Other Drug Use

Many drugs taken by the mother pass directly to the foetus. Research shows that a mother's use of cigarettes, alcohol, recreational or other drugs during pregnancy may have damaging effects on the unborn child. Medical personnel have established that mothers who smoke during pregnancy are more likely to bear smaller babies. This is a concern because small newborns, usually those weighing less than five pounds, tend to be at risk for learning disabilities. Up to 33% of children born between 32 and 35 weeks gestation and up to 25% of LBW babies (< 2000 g) are at risk for school difficulties into late childhood, even when not neurologically impaired. Children born preterm, small for gestational age or with very low birth weight (<1500 g), tend to have the poorest cognitive abilities (Karande and Kulkarni, 2005)

Alcohol also is presumed to be dangerous to the foetus' developing brain and may distort the developing neurons. Serious alcohol abuse during pregnancy has been related to foetal alcohol syndrome which causes low birth weight, intellectual impairment and hyperactivity. Any alcohol use during pregnancy, however, may influence the child's development and lead to problems with learning, attention, memory, or problem solving.

Current research suggests that drug abuse is a possible cause of receptor damage which seems to affect the normal development of brain receptors. Experts propose that the imperfection in the receptors is the reason children with learning disabilities have difficulty in understanding speech sounds.

Problems during Pregnancy or Delivery

Complications during pregnancy are also possible causes of learning disabilities. One for example is when the mother's immune system reacts to the foetus' and treats it as if it is a virus; causing the newly formed brain cells to settle in the wrong part of the brain. Secondly, if during delivery, the umbilical cord becomes twisted and temporarily cuts off oxygen to the foetus can impair brain functions and lead to learning disabilities.

Poor nourishment

Poor nutrition early in life may also lead to learning disabilities later in life. It has been observed that malnutrition has been found to decrease the number of certain nerve and brain cells. Studies show that cognitive development can be impaired when there are low iron blood levels (Cook, et al, 1994). Deficiencies in vitamin B, particularly vitamin B_1 and choline may also be involved. Toxic heavy metals such as cadmium and lead can accumulate in the body and cause hyperactive behavior in some susceptible children.

Toxins in the child's environment

ADD/hyperactivity has been particularly connected with food allergies and chemical allergies. Certain allergy medications have been reported to have adverse side effects on learning and behavior because they affect the central nervous system. The use of some anti-asthma drug has been significantly correlated with reports of inattentiveness, hyperactivity, irritability, drowsiness and withdrawal behavior, these negative side effects being directly proportional to the length of use. The use of these medications may also cause learning disabilities. Some drugs used to treat asthma, allergic rhinitis and other allergic conditions, unfortunately, have a direct and indirect impact on the central nervous system. They have been documented to cause a change in brain electrical activity, mood changes, and changes in sleep patterns, increased irritability and even psychotic reactions.

A history of allergies has been reported by many authors for behavioral problems like being over talkative, irritable, inattentive/distractible, hyperactive, impulsive, and difficult to handle, drowsy/sleepy and withdrawn.

Children on constant steroids for at least a year have been reported to have lower performance on standardized academic achievement tests for reading, verbal memory and mathematics. Over the counter antihistamines have been reported to cause slower reaction time on visual-motor tasks, worsened attention and cerebral processing speed and drowsiness in children; they can be of significant concern to parents of children with learning disabilities.

In addition, there is growing evidence that learning problems may develop in children with cancer who had been treated with chemotherapy or radiation at an early age. This seems particularly true of children with brain tumors who received radiation to the skull.

All the above stated studies and researches do not conclude that learning disabled students cannot learn. They only conclude that the brain of the learning disabled child is wired differently and shows a variance. Learning disabled students can learn, but they must learn in different ways and possibly with different areas of the brain (Fiedorowicz, 2005).

CHAPTER 4

THE CHARACTERISTICS OF LEARNING DISABILITIES

This chapter traces the characteristics of learning disabilities. It answers the question: Whether or not there are distinct signs of learning disabilities? Can these distinctions enable a layman to identify whether or not a child has the probability of learning disabilities?

Understanding the characteristic of learning disabilities is important as it enables us to discern that the child concerned is experiencing a problem in learning. This in turn can enable the caretaker to seek timely professional intervention.

Parents are generally concerned when their children do not study and /or get poor marks in school. Additionally when a friend's child has been diagnosed with a learning disability they are concerned and ask, does my child also have a learning disability? What are the signs and symptoms that can enable a layman to recognize whether a child has a learning disability or not. Are there any distinctive signs?

The answer to these questions is yes, there are particular signs. However, the signs should not be taken as the final diagnoses. If one suspects that a child has learning disabilities it is extremely important to take an expert's opinion. This is because all underachieving children are not learning disabled.

There is ample research done in learning disability that sometimes it is difficult to keep up. Additionally, detection of learning disabilities remains extremely difficult. Also, currently the diagnosis of learning disabilities cannot be definite until the child is in standard/grade 2 or 3, or about eight to nine years old. However, it is important to identify learning disabilities early, rather than when chronic poor school performance becomes evident and also when the secondary problems like emotional disorders arise. Moreover, the longer the children stay with learning disabilities, at any level of severity going without identification, the more difficult the task of remediation and the lower the rate of success (Karande and Kulkarni, 2005).

The following is a list of common characteristics of a learning disabled student. These conditions must be persistent over a long period of time. However, presence of these conditions does not necessarily mean a person is learning disabled.

There are 9 major categories of learning disabilities:

1. Visual Problems
2. Auditory Problems
3. Motor Problems
4. Organizational Problems
5. Conceptual Problems
6. Problems in areas of reading, writing, spelling and arithmetic
7. Speech or language impairments
8. Hyperactivity and impulsivity
9. Issues in emotional disturbance

1. Visual Problems

A visual processing, or perceptual, disorder refers to a delayed ability to understand the meaning of information taken in through the eyes. Difficulties with visual processing affect how visual information is interpreted or processed by the brain.

This is distinct from problems involving sight or what is called 'bad eye-sight'.

Spatial relation

This refers to the position of objects in space. It also refers to the ability to accurately perceive objects in space with reference to other objects.

Visual discrimination

Visual discrimination also refers to the ability to recognize an object as distinct from its surrounding environment. The ability to recognize distinct shapes from their background, such as objects in a picture, or letters on a chalkboard is largely a function of visual discrimination.

This is the ability to differentiate objects based on their individual characteristics. Attributes which children use to identify different objects include: color, form, shape, pattern, size, and position.

Visual closure

Visual closure is often considered to be a function of visual discrimination. This is the ability to identify or recognize a symbol or object when the entire object is not visible.

2. Auditory Problems

An auditory processing disorder interferes with an individual's ability to analyze or make sense of information taken in through the ears. This is different from problems connected to deafness. Difficulties with auditory processing do not affect what is heard by the ear, but do affect how this information is interpreted, or processed by the brain.

Auditory discrimination

Auditory discrimination is the ability to recognize differences in phonemes (sounds). This includes the ability to identify words and sounds that are similar and those which are different.

Auditory memory

Auditory memory is the ability to store and recall information which was given verbally. An individual with difficulties in this area may not be able to follow instructions given verbally or may have trouble recalling information from a story read aloud.

Auditory sequencing

Auditory sequencing is the ability to remember or reconstruct the order of items in a list or the order of sounds in a word or syllable. One example is saying or writing 'ephelant' for 'elephant.'

Auditory blending

Auditory blending is the process of putting together phonemes to form words. For example, the individual phonemes 'c', 'a', and 't' are blended to from the word, 'cat'.

3. Motor Problems

Another brain processing disorder relates to a Motor Coordination Disorder (Sensory Integration Disorder). Some might have difficulty coordinating teams of small muscles (fine motor skills), resulting in poor handwriting and possibly difficulty with buttoning, zipping, or tying. Others might have problems coordinating teams of large muscles (gross motor skills), resulting in being clumsy or running with poor coordination. Some might have difficulty coordinating eye-hand activities (catching, hitting, throwing) or knowing where they are in space, bumping into things. Another aspect of motor problems might relate to balance, resulting in difficulty of riding a bike or quickly going downstairs. Finally, some with motor problems might be very sensitive to touch (tactile sensitivity).

4. Organizational Problems

A child might have difficulty organizing materials, losing, forgetting, or misplacing papers, notebooks, or homework assignments. Or, the problems might be related to organizing ideas when speaking or when writing. This may be revealed as a disorderly work space, or an inability to write a well-planned paragraph on one specific topic. Some might have problems organizing time. They have difficulty with projects due at a certain time, completing test papers or with being on time.

5. Conceptual Problems

A child might have problems in understanding abstract concepts, complex language, consequences and social cues. Conceptual problem concerns a difficulty in interpreting non-verbal language (such as facial expressions or body language) and/ or a difficulty in understanding figures of speech (such as idioms, metaphors or similes).

Children with this problem may also have a problem in anticipating the future (difficulty with predicting consequences) thus they may do something impulsive without considering the consequences. Rigid thinking (unable to see that flexibility is required to deal with a situation, will not 'see' things in shades of grey but only in black and white), poor social skills and peer relations (not maintaining eye contact during a conversation, using an inappropriate tone of voice or language, lacking the social graces) are also affects of conceptual problems.

6. Problems in Areas of Reading, Writing, Spelling and Arithmetic

The 'three Rs-reading,' riting, and 'rithmetic are complex processes. They are so complicated that it is amazing that most of us manage to learn them. Students with academic skills disorders are often years behind their classmates in developing reading, writing, or arithmetic skills. The diagnoses in this category include:

i.   Developmental reading disorder
ii. Developmental writing disorder
iii. Developmental arithmetic disorder

Note: Given that developmental skills build on each other, a person may have more than one learning disability. Moreover, many aspects of speaking, listening, reading, writing, and arithmetic overlap and build on the same brain capabilities. So it is not unexpected that children can be diagnosed as having learning disabilities in more than one area.

Developmental reading disorder

Reading disabilities, also known as dyslexia, is quite widespread. It affects 2 to 18 percent of school-going children. A so called simple act of reading requires mental juggling. It requires a rich, intact network of nerve cells that connect the brain's centers of vision, language, and memory. To read one must simultaneously:

i.   Focus attention on the printed marks and control eye movements across the page
ii. Recognize the sounds associated with letters
iii. Understand words and grammar
iv. Build ideas and images
v.   Compare new ideas to what you already know
vi. Store ideas in memory

A child can have difficulty in any of the tasks involved in reading. However, it is observed that a significant number of children with dyslexia share an inability to distinguish or separate the sounds in spoken words. However, reading is not simply recognizing words. The brain must form images or relate new ideas to those stored in memory to enable the reader to understand or remember the new concepts. If the child is unable to do so then this creates a different reading problem. As a result other types of reading disabilities can appear in the higher standard wherein the focus of reading shifts from word identification to comprehension.

Developmental writing disorder

Writing engages several brain areas and functions. The brain sets up connections for vocabulary, grammar, hand movement and memory. All of which must function in order. A developmental writing disorder may result from problems in any of these areas. A child with a writing disability, particularly an expressive language disorder, might be unable to compose complete grammatical sentences.

Developmental arithmetic disorder

Reflect on the steps one takes to solve a simple arithmetic problem and you will understand that it is a complex process.

Maths involves:

- Recognizing numbers and symbols
- Memorizing facts such as the multiplication table, or Maths procedures to solve certain problems
- Aligning numbers
- Understanding abstract concepts like place value and fractions

Any of these may be difficult for children with developmental arithmetic disorders. Problems with numbers or basic concepts are likely to become evident in the early school years. Disabilities that emerge in the higher standards are more often connected to problems in reasoning.

7. Speech or Language Impairments

Speech and language problems are commonly the first signs of a learning disability. Children with developmental speech and language disorders have difficulty producing speech sounds, using spoken language to communicate, or understanding what other people say. Depending on the problem, the specific diagnosis may be:

- Developmental articulation disorder
- Developmental expressive language disorder
- Developmental receptive language disorder

Developmental articulation disorder

Children with this disorder may have trouble controlling their rate of speech. There may be a delay in learning to make speech sounds. Developmental articulation disorders are common. Fortunately, articulation disorders can often be outgrown or successfully treated with speech therapy. Some children have trouble understanding certain aspects of speech.

Developmental expressive language disorder

Children with language impairments have problems expressing themselves in speech.

Developmental receptive language disorder

Some children have trouble understanding certain aspects of speech. Their hearing is fine, but they cannot make sense of certain sounds, words, or sentences they hear. When children begin schooling some incorrect use of sounds, words, or grammar is a normal part of learning to speak, only when these problems continue that there is any cause for concern.

8. Hyperactivity and Impulsivity

Some children have a type of disorder that leaves them unable to focus their attention. A few children and adults who have attention disorders appear to day-dream excessively. And once you get their attention, they are often easily distracted and tend to mentally drift off into a world of her own. By adolescence, physical hyperactivity usually subsides into fidgeting and restlessness. However, the problems with attention and concentration often continue into adulthood. At work, adults with Attention Deficit Hyperactivity Disorder (ADHD) often have trouble organizing tasks or completing their work. They do not seem to listen to or follow directions. Their work may be messy and appear careless.

Attention disorders, with or without hyperactivity, are not considered learning disabilities in themselves. However, because attention problems can seriously interfere with school performance, they often accompany academic skills disorders.

9. Issues in Emotional Disturbance

This disability is usually manifest in the secondary school. Its basis is usually as a result of repeated failure to achieve the grades that are equivalent to the child's intelligence. This is a distinctive disorder produced by the error of the parents and teachers to understand the child's problems. The indicators like impulsivity, explosive behavior and below age level social competence and mood swings must be present for a period of time effecting emotional functioning.

8. Hyperactivity and Impulsivity

9. Issues in Emotional Disturbance

CHAPTER 5

THE DIFFERENT LEARNING DISABILITIES

The function of perception is to enable an individual to react effectively to their environment. This chapter is included to enable the understanding of Perception and the role it plays in gaining information, learning, understanding and organising thoughts. This in turn facilitates an easier route to understanding the problems faced by the learning disabled.

Perception

Perception refers to the way the world looks, sounds, feels, tastes and smells. In other words perception refers to what is immediately experienced by a person. Perception (how things seem) is a crucial factor in determining behavior. Some of the perceptions are directly tied to information in the sensory channels. However, the sensory information merely provides 'raw data' for much of perception. The data provided is combined with previous information and with thought to create the world we actually experience. In other words when cognitive processes are at work a part of what is perceived comes through the senses from the object before us and another part always comes 'out of our own head'.

At any given moment our sense organs are bombarded by a multitude of stimuli yet we perceive only a few of them clearly. We perceive others less clearly while the rest form a sort of hazy background in our awareness. That is to say we attend to only a few of the events taking place. So attention is a vital factor in perception.

The sensory inputs that people are constantly receiving come into their awareness as shapes, patterns and forms. People do not ordinarily perceive the world around them in patches of colors, variations in brightness or sounds. They see the table floor, walls and trees; they hear automobile horns, footsteps and words.

Perhaps the most fundamental process is the form of recognition of a figure on a ground. We see the object forms of everyday experiences as standing out from the background. Pictures hang on the wall just as words are seen on the page. In these cases the picture and the word are perceived as figures while the wall and the page are the 'ground'. The ability to distinguish an object from its general back ground is basic to all forms of perception.

Organisation of Perception

When several objects are present in the visual field we tend to perceive them as organised into patterns or groupings. Organisation in perception partially explains our perception of complex patterns as unitary forms or objects. We see objects as objects only because grouping processes operate in perception. Without them the various objects and patterns–like a face on the TV screen, a car, or a tree–we perceive would not 'hang together' as objects or patterns. They would merely be so many contoured dots or lines or blotches.

Laws of organisation

Gestalt psychology was founded by German thinkers Max Wertheimer, Wolfgang Kohler, and Kurt Koffka and focused on how people interpret the world. The German word Gestalt means 'structured whole'.

According to Gestalt psychology, the whole is different than the sum of its parts. Based upon this belief, Gestalt psychologists developed a set of principles to explain perceptual organization, or how smaller objects are grouped to form larger ones. These principles are often referred to as the 'laws of perceptual organization.'

However, it is important to note that while Gestalt psychologists call these phenomena 'laws' a more accurate term would be 'principles of perceptual organization.' These principles are much like heuristics, which are mental shortcuts for solving problems.

Law of proximity

A Gestalt principle of organization which maintains that objects or events that are near to one another (in space or time) are perceived as belonging together as a unit or forming an organised group. Even if the shapes, sizes, and objects are radically different, they will appear as a group if they are close together. It is called 'grouping'. The theory is related to the effect created when the collective presence of the set of elements becomes more meaningful than their presence as separate elements. Elements which are grouped together create the illusion of shapes in space, even if the elements are not touching. Grouping of this sort can be achieved with: tone value, color, shape, size and other physical attributes.

Arranging words into sentences or titles is an obvious way to group unrelated elements to enhance their meaning (it also depends on a correct order for comprehension).

Law of similarity

Law of similarity holds that parts of a stimulus field that are similar to each other tend to be perceived as belonging together as a unit. Below, instead of perceiving 36 dots we see three columns of white dots and three columns of black dots.

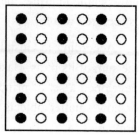

Law of continuation

Law of continuation maintains that there is an inherent tendency to perceive a line as continuing its established direction. This Gestalt law states that learners 'tend to continue shapes beyond their ending points'. The example illustrates that learners are more apt to follow the direction of an established pattern rather than deviate from it. Thus, we perceive the figure as two crossed lines instead of 4 lines meeting at the center.

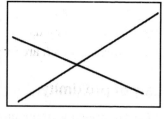

Law of common fate

Law of common fate suggests that aspects of perceptual field that move or function in a similar manner will be perceived as a unit. Like when we see 'serial lighting' or the illustration.

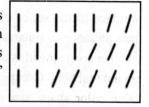

Law of proximity or nearness

Law of proximity or nearness states that objects near each other tend to be seen as a unit. According to this law, the arrangement below (b) is not seen as a rectangle but rather as a set of columns. We tend to perceive items that are near each other as groups.

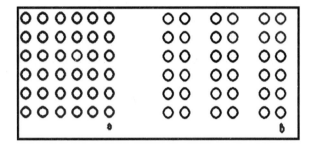

Law of closure

Law of closure proposes that there is an innate tendency to perceive incomplete objects as complete and to close or fill gaps and to perceive asymmetric stimuli as symmetric. Closure is the effect of suggesting a visual connection or continuity between sets of elements which do not actually touch each other in a 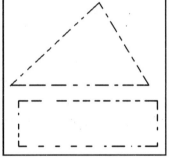 composition. The law of closure makes our perceived world of form more complete, than the sensory stimulation present. The principle of closure applies when we tend to see complete figures even when part of the information is missing. For example in the drawing below, we tend to see a triangle and a rectangle even though the lines are not connected to make a perfect triangle and rectangle.

Visual perception is the ability to recognise, interpret and organise visual images. The activities listed here will help develop visual perception skills and can be incorporated into lessons to benefit all pupils.

Pupils who have difficulties in this area may have:

i.   A poor sense of direction
ii.   Difficulties with organisational skills
iii.   Reverse words in both reading and spelling (e.g. saw for was)
iv.   Difficulty understanding abstract Maths concepts, particularly in the areas of shape, space and measure
v.   Problems with comparative language (e.g. taller than, shorter than, longer than)
vi.   Difficulty in completing jigsaw puzzles
vii.   Problems with copying from the board
viii. Problems with interpreting and organising diagrams, charts, graphs, maps and other visual methods of recording
ix.   Difficulties in judging speed and distance
x.   Difficulty with letter and number orientation
xi.   Difficulty with structuring and organising written work
xii.   Strengths in logic, verbal and non-verbal reasoning
xiii. A leaning towards using multi-sensory strategies when learning
xiv.   A preference for a phonic approach for learning to read

Dyslexia

This section deals with the most familiar learning disability–Dyslexia. The name Dyslexia is often used in place of the word learning disability; however that is an incorrect usage. All learning disabilities are not dyslexia and at the same time dyslexia does not exemplify all learning disabilities.

In this section as in all the rest of the sections in Chapter 5 the characteristics of the disability are described, so are the causes and the disability is detected and diagnosed.

Read the following paragraph:

paragraph	**out**		**you**	**ual**
This	**is ad**	**reading**	**when learning**	**bisabiling**
to vis	peroeplute	bisabilitj.	ntenc	have
This	**paragrabh**	**contains s ix**	**se**	**ces. Eaod**
one bemnonstarles the	dif	a persons with learning
ficulty	dizadititiez	has	when th	eba.
T	**he y yam**	**rot b e**	**low**	**the**	**lines**
ey r	able lo fol	on the pag e. They may ton ed adle
otsee	the letters	the same sa yuo or me. ry diffi
It	**si ve**	**cult wenh teh tea**	**ts pressure on ouy anb**
yo	cher pu	u hvea oj rade ni rfont	fo teh calss.

Is this what you read?

This paragraph is about reading when you have a learning disability or visual perceptual disability.

This paragraph contains six sentences. Each one demonstrates the difficulty a person with learning disabilities may have when they read.

They may not be able to follow the lines on the page. They may not be able to see the letters the same as you or me.

It is very difficult when the teacher puts pressure on you and you have to read in front of the class. (Smith, 1999).

She reads 'saw' for 'was' and 'me' for 'we'.

He says a p instead of a q

He skips, omits, or adds words when he reads out aloud.

She writes 52 for 25.

He thinks 1 2 3 and 123 are the same.

She cannot make out the difference between + and x.

She reads OIL for 710.

Have you met a child who does one or more of the above?

Students, who have the confusion represented by the above examples, have a learning disability with the written language, particularly in reading. Students with such a learning disability might interchange letters within the words when reading, confuse letters such as b, d, p, and q, and have difficulty grasping sound-letter associations in words. Letter and number reversals are the most common warning sign of a learning disability. Such reversal is fairly common up to 7 or 8 years of age and usually reduces by that time. If they do not, it may be appropriate to test for dyslexia.

Dyslexia is a type of reading disability. The word 'dyslexia' comes from 'dys' means 'difficulty' and 'lexia' means 'words'. The combination of which implies 'difficulty with words'. Dyslexia is a disorder that affects millions of people all over the world. It is one type of specific learning disability that affects a person's ability to read.

The definition of Dyslexia is: a specific learning difficulty which mainly affects the development of literacy and language related skills. It is likely to be present at birth and its effects are life-long. It is characterised by difficulties with phonological processing, rapid naming, working memory, processing speed, and the automatic development of skills that may not match up to an individual's other cognitive abilities. The incidence of dyslexia in primary school children in India has been reported to be 2-18 % (Kulkarni and Karande, 2005).

Characteristics

Characteristics of students with dyslexia include:

- Normal intelligence ranges
- Normal articulation and communication but with reading, writing, and spelling levels below average
- Usually perform badly in written-language tests and perform better when verbal tests are carried out
- Usually poor academic achievement due to reading and writing problems
- Learn best through hands-on experience, demonstrations, experimentation, observation, presentations and visual aids
- Labelled as lazy, dumb, careless, immature or as having a behavioral problem. These students, whose disability only affects their reading, might also be labelled as 'not behind enough' to receive additional help
- May be easily frustrated and emotional about school reading or testing
- Might try to hide their reading weaknesses with ingenious compensatory 'strategies'
- May have poor self-esteem
- Have problems with paying attention in a school setting
- Usually show talents in other areas such as art, drama, music, sports, mechanics, story-telling or designing

To understand dyslexia better we first need to understand 'Reading'. Reading is a two way process involving recognition of word (decoding the language) and understanding its meaning (the language comprehension).

Reading is a thinking process. Reading is predominantly considered the most important skill developed during school years. Difficulties in reading actually serve as a common denominator for the lack of success in many other curricular areas.

The Nature of Reading

Reading, a visual auditory task, involves obtaining meaning from symbols (letters and words). It is a learning that is indispensable in this day and age. We are born with skills to listen, hear and see. However, reading is a learnt skill; learning to write and read is not in our genes. Unlike speaking and hearing we have to be taught reading. Linguists believe that the spoken word is 100,000 years old but the written word is only 5, 000 years old. Therefore 'reading' as a skill is only 5, 000 years old (Kantrowitz and Underwood, 1999).

There are four steps in reading:

1. Perception
2. Comprehension
3. Reaction
4. Integration

The first step is recognition. It is the ability to pronounce the word and attach meaning to it.

The second step is the ability which makes the individual words construct a useful idea.

The third step requires judgement action or attaching a feeling to what the author has said.

The final step is the crucial one, the ability to assimilate this idea into the background of experience so it becomes a part of the total experience of the individual.

To sum it up the processes relevant to reading include *phonological, orthographic, rapid automatic naming or RAN, morphological, and receptive and expressive language* (Berninger, Smith and O'Donnell 2004).

The Development of Reading

The purpose of reading is to gather meaning from the printed page. However, the task cannot be accomplished unless an individual can recognize the words that comprise the reading passage and comprehend the meaning behind the word. Learning reading involves five stages:

1. Reading readiness

Reading readiness – serves as a foundation for subsequent growth in reading.

This stage occurs from birth to 6 years of age. The most important factors that contribute to reading readiness are mental maturity, visual abilities, auditory abilities, speech and language development, thinking skills, physical fitness and motor development. Material and teaching approaches tend to be informal at this stage.

During the pre-primary school years the child learns to discriminate shapes, size and color and also manage visual tracking from left to right eye-hand motor coordination. The child also learns to follow instructions, directions and learns to listen. These are the basic skills required to read. Children who demonstrate problems in matching shapes, sizes and objects will later have difficulty in reading. These children may also have problem in distinguishing animal sounds, loud and soft sounds and sounds of vehicles.

2. Initial stage

This period is usually characterised by instructions in sounds-symbol relationship and in decoding words. The emphasis is mostly on building basic sight vocabulary developing confidence in reading situation and beginning instruction in work analysis skills.

3. Rapid development of reading skills

A thorough grounding in the basic reading skills is usually provided at this stage, which normally occurs in the 2nd and 3rd Grade/Std. Major emphasis include sight word vocabulary, improving reading comprehension, increasing competency in independent work analysis, building interest in reading and beginning of widening reading by the use of a variety of material.

4. Wide reading stage

The emphasis at this stage, which typically occurs during intermediate grades is on independent reading with continuing expansion of vocabulary, further development of comprehension skills and constant review of work analysis.

5. Refinement of reading

This stage occurs in junior and senior schools and is characterized by advanced comprehension and study skills along with increased proficiency in reading for different purposes at varying rates.

Reading Skills

A child should be able to follow the language he is going to read. Learning to read is a graded skill arranged in layers. One skill has to be learnt first before it becomes possible to acquire subsequent skills. If the words are written in English, and the child only knows his mother-tongue and not English he will not be able to read what is written. If a child's knowledge of English is poor, then his reading will also be poor. Without improving his English, the reading ability of the child will not improve.

The English language learner has his task made more difficult as English has an irregular orthography. In English, there are 1,120 ways of representing 44 sounds (phonemes) using different letter combinations (graphemes). Mapping letters to word sounds is ambiguous; this is exemplified by pairs of words such as mint/pint, cow/bow (as in bow and arrow), clove/love, where you can only read each pair correctly if you have previously learnt how they should sound (American Association for the Advancement of Science, 2001).

However, there is more to reading than recognizing words. If the brain is unable to form images or relate new ideas to those stored in memory, the reader cannot understand or remember the new concepts. So other types of reading disabilities can appear in the upper grades when the focus of reading shifts from word identification to comprehension.

The next layer or step in reading is concerned with cognitive skills and can be further divided into three steps: *Reception, decoding and learning.*

Reception

The first factor that is concerned with receiving a word is that a child must be able to focus his attention on the written word and to keep his attention on it for some length of time. In other words he must *concentrate* on the word.

The next aspect in receiving the written word is that it must be perceived. In other words, *perception* must take place. Before one can learn anything, one has to become conscious of it through one of the senses. Subsequently one has to *interpret* whatever one has seen or heard. Since reading is directly concerned with our eyes, visual perception plays the most important role in the reading act.

When someone is reading, visual *discrimination* must take place. Color, foreground and background, form, size and position are important aspects of visual discrimination.

1. Color– All printed letters are set against a certain background. The color of the background and letters must be different to set the letters off.
2. Foreground-background–A particular letter or word or sentence, focused on is in the foreground, whereas everything else within the field of vision of the reader (the rest of the page and the book, the desk on which the book is resting, the section of the floor and/or wall that is visible) is consigned to the background.
3. Form or shape–The alphabets all differ in shapes/ form and must be differentiated accordingly. The 26 letters of the English alphabet have capitals and corresponding lower–case equivalents, some of which have a different form.
4. Size–Some lower case and upper-case alphabets look the same but differ in size.
5. Positions– A word is made up of a number of letters arranged in a particular sequence. The reader must therefore be able to discriminate the letters in terms of their *positions*.
6. Dimensionality– If there is a picture included in the text the reader must be able to discriminate *dimensionality*.

After having discriminated every letter in terms of color, foreground and background, form, size and position, letters must be merged into words. The reader must be able to perceive individual parts as a whole. In other words, he must be able to *synthesize*. Although the ability to analyze, that is to perceive the whole in its individual parts, does play a role in reading, this ability is of special importance in spelling.

The above procedures sound very complex, and indeed must be acknowledged as that. In reality they take place all the time at lightning speed while a person is reading. A good reader is unaware of these events because they have been automatic.

Decoding

When an individual attempts to speak a language that has not yet become spontaneous, she will necessarily have to divide her attention between the content of the message and the language itself. She will therefore speak haltingly and with great difficulty. Similarly a person, in whom the above-mentioned foundational skills of reading have not yet become impromptu, will, also read haltingly and with great difficulty. Decoding is a very vital aspect of the reading act. The reader who has weak reading skills has to use a lot of his energy for the reception of the written word, and thus has no or very little energy left to decode it. Without being able to decode the written word, the reader cannot understand it. This explains why some children 'read' without understanding what they are reading.

Decoding means that the reader is able to put down meaning to it. To make this possible first the reader must integrate what he is reading with his existing knowledge and past experiences. Classification is directly connected to reading as is integration. When we see a strange looking plant, a plant like we have never seen before, we still recognize it as a plant. This is because we are familiar with the classification called 'plant'. This implies that, whenever a name is ascribed to an object, it is thereby put into a specific class of objects.

The Gestalt principle of closure is very important in reading. This principle insinuates that the mind is able to draw meaning from objects or pictures that do not look as if full. I -m s-re th-t y-- w-ll b- -ble to und-rsta-d th-s s-ntenc- (I am sure that you will be able to understand this sentence), although more than 25 percent of the letters have been omitted. The mind is able to fill in the gaps that are left in the sentence. The idea of closure is, however, more than just seeing parts of a word and adding details to them.

Closure is also concerned with comprehension. It results in the clarification of the author's message. For example when a writer describes a scene, closure and thus comprehension enables us to 'see' what is happening as described by the author. It would not be possible for the author to relate everything; we are presented with a limited cross-section of reality. It is ultimately up to us to expand and comprehend and complete the picture in our mind.

Last but not the least, imagination plays a role in decoding. While reading, we are also picturing the objects and ideas symbolized by the words. For example when we read a writer's description of a well dressed beautiful girl, we actually imagine or 'see' this beautiful girl with the mind's eye. This performs a vital role in decoding the written word.

Dimensions of Reading

1. Reading is a social process(negative factors such as broken homes, second language, conflicting cultural values between home and school affect reading)
2. Reading is a psychological process. How one feels about ones self affects reading.
3. Reading is a physiological process. One must focus on the printed letters, move along the line, make a return, sweep to note likenesses and differences to discriminate figure-ground relationship. One needs skills in auditory-discrimination, verbal expression, syntactical maturing, eye-hand coordination and motor skills to execute all the mechanical skills associated with reading.
4. Reading is a perceptual process. It utilises perceptual clues, size, shape combination of letters and sound, figure –ground relationship, relationship of the part of the whole sequencing and ordering.

5. Reading is a linguistic process. It requires mastery of phoneme-graphemes relationship, understanding intonations stresses, pauses and tone sequences. Reading depends on understanding the contextual meaning.
6. Reading is an intellectual process. It depends on vocabulary, verbal reasoning, perceiving relationships, memory, and critical judgement.

Thus the child should:

1. Be able to follow the language he is going to read
2. Build up his vocabulary
3. Comprehend what he is reading; if he does not he will soon get bored.
4. Have sitting tolerance
5. Not have vision, hearing and speech problems; all of which should be checked when a child has a reading problem
6. Be motivated at home and school

Analysing Problem of Poor Reading

There are at least 20 factors in a child's make-up or social background which can influence his reading abilities. They fall into 3 distinct groups.

Within the child	Within the family	Within the school
Age	Absenteeism	Inadequate teaching
Dyslexia	English (2nd Language)	
Emotional Difficulty	Disrupted family life	
Sociability	Illiteracy of parents	
Intelligence	Recent immigration	
Motivation	Disrupted schooling	
Perception	Poor stimulation at home	
Hearing	Trauma	
Speech	Unpunctuality	
Vision		

The Types of Reading Problems

Researchers have identified three kinds of developmental reading disabilities that often overlap but that can be separate and distinct:

- Phonological deficit, pointing to a basic problem in the phonological processing system of oral language.

- Processing speed/orthographic processing deficit, affecting speed and accuracy of printed word recognition (also called naming speed problem or fluency problem).

- Comprehension deficit, often coinciding with the first two types of problems, but specifically found in children with social-linguistic disabilities (e.g., autism spectrum), vocabulary weaknesses, generalized language learning disorders, and learning difficulties that affect abstract reasoning and logical thinking. The main reasons for reading problems are auditory perception difficulties, visual perception difficulties, language processing difficulties. However sometimes ineffective reading instruction is also a problem.

Visual perception difficulties

A visual processing, or perceptual, disorder refers to a hindered ability to make sense of information taken in through the eyes. This is different from problems involving sight or sharpness of vision. Difficulties with visual processing affect how visual information is interpreted or processed by the brain.

Visual discrimination

This is the ability to differentiate objects based on their individual characteristics. Visual discrimination is vital in the recognition of common objects and symbols. Attributes which children use to identify different objects include: color, form, shape, pattern, size, and position. Visual discrimination also refers to the ability to recognize an object as distinct from its surrounding environment.

In terms of reading, visual discrimination difficulties can interfere with the ability to accurately identify symbols, gain information from pictures, charts, or graphs, or be able to use visually presented material in a productive way. One example is being able to distinguish between m, n, h, where the only distinguishing feature is the number of humps in the letter. Pupils with difficulties in this area confuse letters with similar configuration like – h and n, i and j, u and w or might be unable to distinguish visually between words like nip and nap.

The ability to recognize distinct shapes from their background, such as objects in a picture, or letters on a board is largely a function of visual discrimination

Children with Visual Disabilities may demonstrate the following:

1. Difficulty with visual memory and visualization
2. Usually rather slow to begin reading (help them to sound out as they go along)
3. Difficulty retaining spelling rules and unusually spelled words (they spell phonetically)
4. Copying from the blackboard or any source for that matter is wrought with mistakes
5. The image is forgotten between taking it in and transposing it
6. Difficulty in checking their own work due to problems retaining correct image
7. Difficulty in problem solving due to problems visualizing scenarios in their mind
8. Difficulty in visualizing the end result and thereby becoming stuck in the middle of tasks
9. Tendency towards concrete thinking; concrete thinking is thinking characterized by immediate experience; abstract

thinking is a level of thinking about things that is removed from the facts of the 'here and now'. For example a concrete thinker will think about this particular plant and the abstract thinker can and will think about plants in general.

10. Difficulty with spatial relationships such as distance, size, shape and how things fit together to form a whole
11. Difficulty estimating passage of time
12. Difficulty with a sense of direction
13. They sometimes appear to others 'self-absorbed' or 'out to lunch'
14. Difficulty being socially aware; they miss interpersonal cues and are usually the last to know how someone is feeling also fail to pick up on what is and isn't 'cool'
15. These children need the most support in elementary school when they need to understand, manipulate and build on visual symbols the most.

Phonological awareness

Phonological awareness is the understanding that language is made up of individual sounds (phonemes) which are put together to form the words we write and speak. This is a fundamental precursor to reading. Children who have difficulty with phonological awareness will often be unable to recognize or isolate the individual sounds in a word, recognize similarities between words (as in rhyming words), or be able to identify the number of sounds in a word. These deficits can affect all areas of language including reading, writing, and understanding of spoken language.

Though phonological awareness develops naturally in most children, the necessary knowledge and skills can be taught through direct instruction for those who have difficulty in this area.

Auditory discrimination

Auditory discrimination is the ability to detect similarities and differences when listening to sounds or the ability to recognize differences in phonemes (sounds). One of the characteristics of students with auditory discrimination problems in reading is an inability to differentiate between phonetic sounds.

Children with disturbance in this area may have:

1. Problems identifying speech sounds
2. Poor listening skills, especially when there is background noise
3. Difficulty discriminating between similar words
4. Difficulty with rhyming activities
5. Poor articulation of sounds and words

Auditory memory

Auditory memory is the ability to store and recall information which was given verbally. An individual with difficulties in this area may not be able to follow instructions given verbally or may have trouble recalling information from a story read aloud.

The difficulty in recalling specific sounds and names may explain the substitutions which the learning disabled make, as, for example, dad for father or baby for daughter. Not only are the substituted words easier to pronounce, but their pronunciation is based on regular phonics principles while the others are not. Pronunciation of words like father, daughter etc., requires the child to remember the irregularities in making symbol-sound associations.

Auditory sequencing

Auditory sequencing is the ability to remember or reconstruct the order of items in a list or sequence of sounds long enough to reproduce them in the correct order when reading out loud. The separate letters may be related with their sounds correctly but when the word is pronounced putting the syllables together the child mixes up the order. For example ephelant in place of elephant. The child may mix up compound words, for example mindwill instead of windmill, cornpop for popcorn.

Sound blending

Sound blending is the ability to synthesie sounds into complete words. For example, the individual phonemes c -kuh a- aah   t- aah are blended to form the word, cat. Most individuals understand this, but dyslexics can hear only 'cat'—one sound. Because of this they cannot sound out words, the first step in reading. Most children easily understand and grasp this sounding-out phase and quickly this process becomes an automatic part of reading. Dyslexics are at a complete loss right from the beginning as they cannot make the connection between the symbol and the sound.

Causes of Dyslexia

The causes for dyslexia are neurobiological and genetic. Research shows that individuals inherit the genetic links for dyslexia (Saviour and Ramachandra, 2006). If one of your immediate family members is dyslexic there are more chances that you could also be dyslexic.

Genetics researcher like Smith (University of Nebraska Medical Center), Centre for Reading Research in Norway (Encyclopedia of Mental Disorders) Javier Gayán of Neocodex, Seville, Spain (Medical News Today, 2009) to name a few suggest that multiple genes contributing to language impairment, some of which also contribute to reading or speech impairment. Through their experiments they have discovered that reading disorders are most likely the result of what is, to all intents and purposes, faulty wiring in the brain and not lethargy, stupidity or a poor home environment. Their work validates that dyslexia is largely inherited. Scientists have identified multiple chromosomes that may be involved. Scientists have also discarded another old stereotype, that dyslexia affects boys more often then girls. Studies indicate that many girls are affected too but they may not be getting help (Kantrowitz and Underwood, 1999).

Using functional Magnetic Resonance Imaging (fMRI) it has been found that people with dyslexia have a deficit in parts of the left hemisphere of the brain involved in reading. In particular, doctors have noticed that the language center in a dyslexic brain showed microscopic differences from non-dyslexic brains, and these differences affect the typical six-layer structure of the cortex. These differences affect connectivity and functionality of the brain in critical areas related to auditory processing and visual processing, which seems consistent with the hypothesis that dyslexia stems from a phonological awareness deficit. In additional research, it has been reported from CAT scan studies that the brains of dyslexic children were 'symmetrical,' unlike the asymmetrical brains of non-dyslexic readers who had larger left hemispheres.

How Dyslexia is Diagnosed

A thorough psycho-educational evaluation is necessary to diagnose dyslexia (or LD) in a child. There are many factors the psychologist or other health professional reviews to diagnose the disability. The testing determines the child's functional reading level and compares it to reading potential, which is evaluated by an intelligence test. All aspects of the reading process are examined to pinpoint where the breakdown is occurring. The testing further assesses how a child takes in and processes information and what the child does with the information. The tests determine whether a child learns better by hearing information (auditory), looking at information (visual), or doing something (kinesthetic). They also assess whether a child performs better when allowed to give information (output), by saying something (oral), or by doing something with their hands (tactile-kinesthetic). The tests also evaluate how all of these sensory systems (modalities) work in conjunction with each other.

The tests administered are standardized and are considered highly reliable. Many of the tests use a game-type or puzzle format which can help make the child feel more comfortable. Children should be well rested prior to the testing and have a good meal. Whether or not the testing is done at school, the parents may want to talk to their child about a new person who will be working with them. However, parents should not try to coach the child concerning the testing. It is recommended that parents not be present during the testing.

A standard battery of tests can include, but is not limited to, the following:

1. Wechsler Intelligence Scale for Children-Third Edition (WISC-III)
2. Kaufman Assessment Battery for Children (KABC)
3. Stanford-Binet Intelligence Scale
4. Woodcock-Johnson Psycho-Educational Battery
5. Peabody Individual Achievement Tests-Revised (PIAT)
6. Wechsler Individual Achievement Tests (WIAT)
7. Kaufman Tests of Educational Achievement (KTEA)
8. Bender Gestalt Test of Visual Motor Perception
9. Beery Developmental Test of Visual-Motor Integration
10. Motor-Free Visual Perception Test
11. Visual Aural Digit Span Test (VADS)
12. Test of Auditory Perception (TAPS)
13. Test of Visual Perception (TVPS)

14. Peabody Picture Vocabulary Test-Revised
15. Expressive One-Word Picture Vocabulary Test
16. Test for Auditory Comprehension of Language

Most Recent Research

Scientists formerly believed that as we aged, the brain's networks cemented in place. However, most up-to-date research suggests that the brain never stops changing and adjusting. Brain Plasticity is the ability of the brain to adapt and reorganize neural pathways as a result of new experiences or learning (Segeklen, 2006). This flexibility can help sustain language processing even when there are serious impediments. This is good news for the dyslexic reader; as this implies that special and effective remedial exercises can take advantage of the brain's adaptive capacities and aid individuals to overcome certain language and reading problems. Now that we understand that the brain is plastic and the earlier we start remediation the better it is for the children.

The challenge is identifying children who might have learning problems as early as possible. Researchers believe that early interventions are most successful. They infer that there's a window between the ages of 5 and 7 when the underlying skills of reading are most effortlessly learned (Kantrowitz and Underwood, 1999) They believe that if children are at risk, start intervention at the kindergarten level. The needs can be addressed with 30 minutes of intervention a day. However, by the time the children are 8 or 9, it takes at least two hours a day of special training. This strongly implies that the key is finding those at risk early.

Dysgraphia

Agatha (Miller) Christie was one of the most famous mystery novel writers. Her writing career spanned over 50 years and she wrote over 100 novels, short stories, and plays. She sold over two billion books worldwide and also received the Order of Dame Commander of the British Empire.

She was able to read by the age of four and grew up to be a voracious reader. However, she was extremely shy causing her parents to worry about her. They believed that she might be developmentally challenged.

'I, myself, was always recognized...as the "slow one" in the family. It was quite true, and I knew it and accepted it. Writing and spelling were always terribly difficult for me. I was...an extraordinarily bad speller and have remained so until this day.'

– Agatha Christie

Despite being a productive author, Agatha was dreadful at spelling and had a terrible handwriting. She actually did not begin to write her books until she could type. She would even dictate her stories to a typist because her handwriting was appalling. She also had a bad memory for numbers and had difficulty adding. It is believed she had dysgraphia or difficulty with written mechanical language, such as spelling and punctuation. Dysgraphia is in addition characterized by poor handwriting. However, Agatha loved to learn and had many interests she indulged, including archaeology and horticulture.

Dysgraphia is a Greek word. The word *'graph'* refers both to the hand's function in writing and to the letters formed by the hand. The prefix *dys* indicates that there is impairment. *'Graph'* refers to producing letter forms by hand. The suffix *'ia'* refers to having a condition.

The word 'Dysgraphia' basically means difficulty expressing thoughts in writing. It is a learning disability that affects writing abilities. It can manifest itself as difficulties with poor handwriting, spelling and trouble putting thoughts on paper. Dysgraphia is a specific learning disability that affects how easily children acquire written language and how well they use written language to express their thoughts. The prevalence of dysgraphia in school going children in India has been reported to be 14% (in Kulkarni and Karande, 2005)

Dysgraphia may exist in isolation but more commonly occurs with other learning difficulties, like dyslexia, aphasia, dyscalculia, and attention deficit disorder with or without hyperactivity.

Given that dysgraphia is a processing disorder, difficulties can change throughout a lifetime. People with dysgraphia often can write and may have a higher than average IQ. However, they lack co-ordination and may find other fine motor tasks such as tying shoes difficult. Still, at the same time it does not affect all fine motor skills. They can also lack basic spelling skills (having difficulties with p,q,b,d), and often will write the wrong word when trying to put together thoughts on paper. In children, the disorder generally emerges when they are first introduced to writing. They make inappropriately sized and spaced letters, or write wrong or misspelled words despite methodical instruction.

Children with the disorder may have other learning disabilities; however, they usually have no social or other academic problems. Cases of dysgraphia in adults generally occur after some neurological trauma or it might be diagnosed in a person with autism and Asperser's Syndrome.

What is Dysgraphia?

- is a processing problem
- is a difficulty in automatically remembering and mastering the sequence of muscle motor movements needed in writing

- causes writing exhaustion
- interferes with communication of ideas in writing
- is the cause of weak organization on the line

Dysgraphia should not be mistaken for:

- Laziness
- Not trying
- Not caring
- Sloppy writing
- General sloppiness
- Careless writing
- Visual-motor delay
  (Richards, 2002)

Signs of Dysgraphia:

- Generally illegible writing (despite appropriate time and attention given to the task)
- Incorrect directionality of letters
- Too much or too little slant
- Mirror writing
- Inconsistencies: mixtures of print and cursive, upper and lower case, or irregular sizes, shapes, or slant of letters
- Unfinished words or letters, omitted words
- Inconsistent position on page with respect to lines and margins
- Inconsistent spaces between words and letters
- Tight, awkward, cramped or unusual grip: holding the writing instrument very close to the paper, holding thumb over two fingers and writing from the wrist ('fisting the pen')
- Gets exhausted due to writing
- Strange wrist, body, or paper position
- Avoiding writing or drawing taskst
- Difficulty organizing thoughts on paper

- Difficulty with syntax structure and grammar
- Talking to self while writing, or carefully watching the hand that is writing
- Legible handwriting but slow speed and laboured copying
- A discrepency between written ideas and understanding. Content which does not reflect the student's other language skills like speech and comprehension
(Jones, 1998, and National Center for Learning Disabilities, 2003)

Research on dysgraphia reveals that there are many variations in its classifications and subtypes. Researchers separate dysgraphia into two classifications: specific and non-specific.

1. Specific dysgraphia is attributed to spelling disabilities, motor coordination, and language disabilities.
2. Non-specific dysgraphia is traced to causes such as retardation, psychosocial insufficiency, or poor attendance at school (Kay, 2004).

Types of Dysgraphia

Dysgraphia is divided into three subtypes: dyslexic, motor, and spatial (Deuel, 1995). The writer suggests that dyslexic is the most commonly noted subtype.

1. **Dyslexic dysgraphia**– In this subtype text that is spontaneously written by the individual is illegible, especially when the text is complex. Oral spelling is poor, but drawing and copying of written text are relatively normal.
2. **Motor dysgraphia**–Dysgraphia caused due to motor clumsiness; text both written by individual automatically and copied is illegible, while oral spelling is normal. Furthermore drawing is usually problematic.

3. **Spatial dysgraphia**–In Dysgraphia caused due to a defect in the understanding of space. Children display illegible writing, whether automatically produced or copied. Oral spelling is normal. Drawing is problematic.

The International Dyslexia Association fact sheet (2008) suggests that dysgraphia can occur with other learning disabilities. Children with impaired handwriting may also have attention-deficit hyperactivity disorder (ADHD)–inattentive, hyperactive, or combined inattentive and hyperactive subtypes. Children with this kind of dysgraphia may respond to a combination of explicit handwriting instruction plus stimulant medication, but appropriate diagnosis of ADHD by a qualified professional and monitoring of response to both instruction and medication are needed.

Dysgraphia may occur alone or with dyslexia (impaired reading disability) or with oral and written language learning disability. As dyslexia is a disorder that includes poor word reading, word decoding, oral reading fluency, and spelling children with dyslexia may have impaired orthographic and phonological coding and rapid automatic naming and switching. Phonological coding refers to coding sounds in spoken words in working memory. Phonological coding is necessary for developing phonological awareness–analyzing the sounds in spoken words that correspond to alphabet letters. If children have both dysgraphia and dyslexia, they may also have difficulty in planning sequential finger movements.

Oral and written language learning disability are disorders of language (morphology–word parts that mark meaning and grammar; syntax–structures for ordering words and understanding word functions; finding words in memory, and/or making inferences that go beyond what is stated in text). These disorders affect spoken as well as written language. Children with these language disorders may also exhibit the same writing and reading and related disorders as children with dysgraphia or dyslexia.

Written Language

There are three parts to written language:

1. Handwriting
2. Spelling
3. Written expression

Disorder in Handwriting

Handwriting aims towards legibility. Handwriting includes tasks such as copying, tracing, scribbling and writing from dictation. The problem arises due to poor sequencing, visual motor integrating, eye-hand coordinating or sometimes poor instructions.

Although most handwriting instruction is the responsibility of the teacher, the child with dysgraphia should be referred to occupational therapists. The therapist's responsibility is to determine underlying postural, motor, sensory-integrative, and perceptual deficits. The therapist also analyzes writing readiness skills, and the sensory-motor, cognitive, psychosocial, and environmental factors that interfere with the development of legible handwriting. A therapist as well as a special educator provides intervention where appropriate, by planning exercises to augment the skills required by the child. Additionally they should determine strategies for the teacher to improve classroom performance and suggest supporting home activities to be carried out with the parents help.

Zaner Bloser Evaluation Scale is used in formal assessment. It assesses both manuscript writing and cursive writing. A sample is taken and compared. In this assessment tool spacing of words, line quality, strokes are evaluated. Being a prescriptive assessment tool it is effective, as it gives directions in planning a remedial program.

Handwriting skill is also related to some perceptual and perceptual-motor skills. Wedell found that young students with handwriting problems had greater difficulties with position in space, drew poorly when drawing required crossing from one side of their bodies to the other, and did not benefit from handwriting tasks as much as other students.

In her book 'Learning Disabilities: Theories, Diagnosis, and Teaching Strategies', Janet Lerner states that some of the underlying shortcomings that interfere with handwriting performance are:

1. Poor motor skills
2. Faulty visual perception of letters and words
3. Difficulty in retaining visual impressions
4. The student's problem may also be in cross-modal transfer from the visual to motor modalities

Experts maintain early treatment can help prevent or reduce many problems. For example, special exercises can increase strength in the hands and improve muscle memory. This is training muscles to remember the shapes of letters and numbers.

Initially, children with impaired handwriting benefit from activities that support learning to form letters:

*   Playing with clay to strengthen hand muscles
*   Keeping lines within mazes to develop motor control
*   Connecting dots or dashes to create complete letter forms
*   Tracing letters with index finger or eraser end of pencil
*   Imitating the teacher modelling sequential strokes in letter formation
*   Copying letters from models

Subsequently, once children learn to form legible letters, they benefit from instruction that helps them develop automatic letter writing, using the following steps to practice each of the 26 letters of the alphabet in a different order daily:

- Studying numbered arrow cues that provide a consistent plan for letter formation
- Covering the letter with a 3 x 5 card and imaging the letter in the mind's eye
- Writing the letter from memory after interval that increases in duration over the handwriting lessons
- Writing letters from dictation (spoken name to letter form)
- Writing letters during composing for 5 minutes on a teacher-provided topic

Disorder in Spelling

Spelling is the opposite of reading. Reading is decoding what is written whereas spelling is encoding. The skills or competencies that are needed in order to spell are the ability to:

1. Read the word
2. Visualise the word (in simple words close your eyes and see the word)
3. Have a phonic capacity to associate the phoneme (sound) with the grapheme (letter)
4. Phonic generalisation
5. Motor facility

What causes spelling difficulty is not exactly known except the fact that words spell and are pronounced differently in the English language. English is a difficult language to learn to spell. It would be much easier if each phoneme had one and only one grapheme. But that is not the case. There are 251 different spellings for the 44 sounds of English and the language contains many irregularly spelled words. What makes spelling even more complicated is that the written form of the English language has an inconsistent pattern; approximately 50% of spellings follow regular phonetic rules.

This makes it difficult for a child with learning disability for the reason that in reading, context and other cues help one to decode a word, however in spelling; one must produce the word after hearing or thinking about it. Spelling requires that a person produce in written or oral form the correct sequence of letters that form a particular word. To do this, a person converts phonemes (sounds) into graphemes (written letters). There is only one correct way to spell any particular word with a given meaning. Thus, spelling does not allow any room for 'creative' or 'imaginative' answers or methods; a word is either spelled correctly or it is misspelled.

The skill of spelling involves many sub skills. The sub skills of particular importance are:

1. The ability to analyze, i.e. to perceive the whole in its individual parts.
2. Auditory perception of letter sounds and auditory memory.
3. Decoding skills.
4. Visual memory for sequences.

Shortcomings in one or more of these sub skills can greatly affect a child's spelling ability.

The types of errors that are committed in spelling are:

• Omission of silent letters (tak for talk)
• Omission of sounded letters(personl for personal)
• Omission of double letter(fil for fill)
• Doubling (untill for until)
• Addition of single letter(backe for bake)
• Transportation (pickel for pickle)
• Phonetic substitution for a vowel (injoy for enjoy)
• Phonetic substitution for a consonant (prizon for prison)
• Phonetic substitution for a syllable (stopt for stopped)
• Phonetic substitution for a word (weary for very)

Strategies for teaching spelling are:

- Be sure
- Practice spelling the word by breaking up the word
- Teach students to use cover-copy-compare method to learn new words
- Have the learner self-correct practice papers noting errors and making corrections
- Provide ample opportunity for students to practice written words
- Be sure learner can pronounce word correctly (should be first)

Disorder in Written Expression

Handwriting is a mechanical task. It is primarily a visual-motor task that does not require complex cognitive abilities. However, written expression offers a visual evidence of how a child can arrange her thoughts and ideas and convey understanding of it. Written expression covers concept development, imagination and comprehension. It is the final component of language to develop and follow listening, reading and writing skills.

Children with expression difficulties can find vital and imperative activities at school such as writing and taking down notes to be an overwhelming problem. Note-taking requires listening comprehension, retaining information while continuing to process new information and summarizing the points. Writing involves an extremely complex neuro-developmental process which engages multiple brain mechanisms. The physical act of writing occurs simultaneously and sequentially with the higher cognitive processes of attention, listening, understanding and memory. All of which must be achieved with adequate speed atomaticity and legible handwriting for the notes to be useful later on. Writing is a complex task requiring the mastery and integration of a number of sub-skills. The process of writing connects cognition, language, and motor skills. Some children have difficulties in one aspect of the process, such as producing legible handwriting or spelling, whereas other children have difficulty organizing and sequencing their ideas.

Seeing that written expression is usually acquired after a child has had extensive experience with reading, spelling and verbal expression these problems are not identified until he reaches the higher standards. This problem usually arises in the 4th or the 5th standard. Disorders of written expression are defined as a combination of difficulties in an individual's ability to compose written text that are made apparent by illegible handwriting, letter shape distortions, dysfluent writing, spelling errors and difficulty in written expression of ideas that cannot be credited to disabilities in reading or oral expression (DSM IV – American Psychiatric Association, 1994). Difficulties in one area can delay skill development in the other areas, as practice of all writing skills may be impeded. Whether written expression exists as an isolated disorder is uncertain. Frequently, writing is the most significant stumbling block for a child. Children often experience this disorder as thoughts move faster than their hand can translate them into written ideas on the page.

Diagnosis

A variety of assessment tools are drawn on when evaluating disorders of written language. These embrace the range of characteristics of the dysgraphic writer, such as writing speed, attention and concentration, writing organization, spelling, knowledge and use of vocabulary and language expression.

Assessment instruments which are used in diagnosing written language disorders include the Processing Speed Index scores from the Wechsler Intelligence Scale for Children-Revised (WISC) (Indian adaptation by MC Bhatt) to determine that the child's level of intellectual functioning was average or above average, the Bender-Gestalt, the Jordan Left-Right Reversal Test was used. A variety of written language achievement measures including the Test of Written Language, the Woodcock-Johnson Psycho-Educational Battery (Revised); includes dictation, proofing, writing fluency, and writing samples subtests for children aged 5 years to adulthood and the Diagnostic Achievement Battery-Second Edition were devised.

How We can Aid a Child with Dysgraphia

Strategies with which to help a student with Dysgraphia achieve success, are divided into three categories:

- **Remediation:** providing instruction for improving handwriting and writing skills

- **Modifications:** altering educational expectations in schools to lessen and/or avoid weakness experienced by the student

- **Accommodations:** providing alternatives to written tasks

Each type of strategy should be considered when planning instruction and support as each one has its own merit and is equally important. An individual with Dysgraphia will benefit from help from class teachers, special educators and family member. Using the most helpful and constructive strategy is a process of trying different ideas and exchanging thoughts on what is most effective.

Continual handwriting practice. Encourage proper grip, posture and paper positioning for writing. It is important to reinforce this early as it is difficult for students to unlearn bad habits later on. Handwriting is an important feature in schooling as all through a student's life they need to write and submit written work for assessment.

Multi-sensory techniques should be utilized for teaching both manuscript and cursive writing. The techniques need to be practiced over a large period of time so that the letters are fairly spontaneous before the student is asked to use these skills to communicate ideas. For example, speaking through motor sequences such as 'b' is 'big stick down, circle away from my body', or practice writing letters and numbers in the air with big arm movements to improve motor memory of these important shapes. Also practice letters and numbers with smaller hand or finger motions.

Be creative and put handwriting instruction into the student's schedule as many students would actually like to have better handwriting.

Encourage the student to use a dictionary or a spellchecker. Additionally have someone else proofread his work.

Help students create a checklist for editing work - spelling, neatness, grammar, syntax, clear progression of ideas.

Encourage students to summarize their thoughts. Then write the extended piece as it is vital to get the main ideas down first. Learning disabled children get distracted when they have to struggle with the spelling, punctuation, and handwriting quality.

Encourage writing practice by using alternative pressure free reasons for writing such as letters, a diary, making household lists or keeping track of sports teams.

Encourage student to talk aloud as they write home work or during remedial. This may provide valuable auditory feedback.

Do homework in a reliable step-wise sequence.

1. Plan the paper
2. Gather the ideas and consider they should be put together
3. Organize the thoughts and ideas first. Make a list of key thoughts and words that will be used in the paper.

4. Write a draft or an outline to be sure to include all the information.
5. Correct the work. Check the work for proper spelling, grammar (use a dictionary or spell-check). Edit the paper to improve subject matter.
6. Revise work, producing a final draft. Read it one last time before submitting it.

If a student becomes tired, try the following:

- Shake hands fast, but not violently. Tell the child to rub hands together and focus on the feeling of warmth.
- Tell the child to rub hands on thighs in circles.
- Perform 'sitting pushups' by placing each palm on the chair with fingers facing forward. Students push down on their hands, lifting their body slightly off the chair

Permit the student to use the writing instrument that is most comfortable for them.

Permit older students to use the line width of their choice. Remember that some students use small writing to mask messiness or spelling uncertainties.

Permit students to use paper or writing instruments of different colors.

Allow student to use graph paper for math, or to turn lined paper sideways to keep columns and rows organized.

If copying is painstaking, allow the student to make editing marks rather than recopying the whole thing.

Allow the student to dictate some assignments or tests to a 'scribe'. Train the 'scribe' to write what the student says verbatim and then allow the student to make changes, without assistance from the scribe.

Allow student to tape record important assignments. Find alternative means of assessing knowledge, such as oral reports or visual projects.

Reduce copying aspects of work; for example, in Math, provide a worksheet with the problems already on it instead of having the student copy the problems.

Allow more time for written tasks including note-taking, copying and tests.

Avoid cutting marks for neatness and/or spelling tests.

Be patient and encourage the student to be patient with himself. Becoming a good writer takes time and practice.

Dyscalculia

Try this and see what the result is:

- When I copy numbers I write them in the wrong order. For example, I write 45 instead of 54.
- When using a phone I dial numbers in the wrong order. I just cannot remember the correct numbers.
- I have difficulty adding up and taking away.
- I do not understand what odd and even numbers mean.
- I do not like shopping as I have problems giving and receiving exact change.
- The 24 hour clock confuses me totally.
- I have a problem with reading of an analogue clock (with hands) and often make mistakes like reading 2.20 pm for 4.10 pm.
- I make mistakes when I subtract larger numbers.
- I have never been able to do 'tables'.
- Sometimes I see signs like + or x and I confuse them and sometimes use + for x or vice versa.
- If someone says 'divide' I cannot visualize the symbol.
- I find it very difficult to copy lots of numbers from a board onto paper. I put them in the incorrect order.
- I never get the right answer even if I use the calculator.
- When I try a Maths problem I often forget half way through what exactly I had to do, and so cannot finish it.
- Sometimes I forget the names of shapes like a square and a rectangle.
- When I work out a Maths question on the page, the working is always very messy because I have to make many corrections
- Often I know the answer to a Maths problem, but cannot explain how I got to that answer.
- I get really confused between the value of large numbers such as 10,050 and 70,540 and I cannot work out which one is larger than the other.

- I do not understand percentages at all!
- I have a difficulty answering problems that make use of words like 'more than', 'lesser than', 'before', 'after', 'greater than' and so on.
- Sometimes when I am faced with a question that has to do with numbers, I just cannot cope and I become very anxious.
- Maths frightens me. I really do not understand it at all

If the answer is 'yes' to half or more of these items there is a possibility that the individual doing the test has 'dyscalculia'. In the case of children the items should be relevant to what is taught in the child's class.

Dyscalculia is made up of 'dys', meaning a form of special difficulties and 'calculus', meaning counting. Dyscalculia refers to difficulties with counting and is a term which is equivalent to dyslexia in the following respect –

Dyslexia–dysfunction in the reception, comprehension, or production of language information.

Dyscalculia–dysfunction in the reception, comprehension, or production of specific mathematical tasks (Science Daily, 2008).

Typically, the child with dyscalculia or a math, disability has trouble making satisfactory progress in mathematics similar to that of her peer group despite the implementation of effective teaching practices over time.

There are many more signs of dyscalculia than the list above in the box. A few more are:

- Difficulty with the abstract concepts of time and direction
- Inability to recall schedules and order of past or future events
- Unable to keep track of time. May be continually late
- Mistaken recollection of names. Poor name or face retrieval. Substitute names beginning with same letter or same sounding names

- Results in addition, subtraction, multiplication and division are inconsistent
- Poor mental math ability
- Poor with money and credit
- Makes silly mistakes when writing, reading and recalling numbers. Has a difficulty with number additions, substitutions, transpositions, omissions, and reversals
- Inability to grasp and remember math concepts, rules, formulas, sequence (order of operations) and basic addition, subtraction, multiplication and division facts
- Finds difficulty in managing money
- Difficulty in processing information presented rapidly and also in distinguishing what is important in a problem
- Problems in the coordination of fine movements and the tendency in writing for letters to be reversed, rotated, unexpectedly large or poorly formed
- Difficulties in games that involve mathematical computations of some sort or the question of whose turn is next, like cards and board games
- Poor ability to 'visualize', like reading maps- the geographical locations of countries, cities, oceans and streets. Problem with diagrams
- Poor long term memory (retention and retrieval) of concept mastery; may be able to perform math operations one day, but draw a blank the next. May be able to do book work but fails all tests and quizzes
- May be unable to comprehend or visualize mechanical processes
- Lack abstract thinking
- Poor memory for the layout of places. Gets lost or disoriented easily. May have a poor sense of direction. Loose things often as they forget where they were placed.

- May have difficulty grasping concepts of formal music education. Difficulty in sight-reading music, learning fingering to play an instrument and so on
- May have poor athletic dexterity
- May have difficulty keeping up with rapidly changing bodily directions like in dance and exercise classes
- Difficulty with train of thoughts; loses track of whose turn it is during games, like cards and board games
- Difficulty remembering dance step sequences and rules of a particular sport
- Difficulty keeping score during games
- Has limited tactical planning ability for games like Chess, Othello, Monopoly and Backgammon

The Term and the Definition

Even though dyscalculia affects about 5-8 % of the school going population the research community has not carried out enough work on it; not as much as on dyslexia. Research into the underlying causes of dyscalculia is currently very much in its infancy. Thus, we do not know enough about dyscalculia in exact details, the role the brain plays in dealing with its various sub-types, its exact diagnosis and remediation.

The terms drawn on for dyscalculia are plenty. Developmental dyscalculia is a term used by Shalev and colleagues (2001) to distinguish it from the acquired kind. However, other studies of selective deficits in numeracy acquisition have used terminology like for example dyscalcula, arithmetic learning disabilities, specific arithmetic difficulties and specific arithmetic learning difficulties.

Strangely, there is no national or international agreement about dyscalculia; there is a range of existing definitions. The definition for dyscalculia used in the USA is: 'dyscalculia is conceptualized as a hereditary disorder, being present from early childhood, and is not the result of poor or inappropriate schooling, cultural factors or medical conditions' (American Psychiatric Association, 2000; WHO, 1996).

The definition used in the UK by the Department for Education and Skills (DfES, 2001, p. 2) is: 'Dyscalculia is a condition that affects the ability to acquire arithmetical skills. Dyscalculic learners may have difficulty understanding simple number concepts, lack an intuitive grasp of numbers, and have problems learning number facts and procedures. Even if they produce a correct answer or use a correct method, they may do so mechanically and without confidence'.

The most up to date, 2007, definition used is : Development dyscalculia could be defined as a dysfunction of developing neural networks specifically for the numerical domain due to a variety of possible reasons, including genetic vulnerability, deficits in domain-general abilities such as visual-spatial and verbal processing or attention and working memory, as well as adverse or maladaptive environmental and psychological conditions, for example, deprivation and anxiety (von Aster and Shalev, 2007).

What all of these definitions have in common is:

1. The presence of difficulties in mathematics
2. Some degree of specificity to these (i.e. the lack of all-inclusive academic difficulties)
3. The theory that these difficulties are caused in some way by brain dysfunction

The Nature of Maths

Most people are so much in awe of Maths that they do not realize that the problem with Maths often arises because the rules of Maths are inconsistent. Many of these inconsistencies are overlooked at the primary stage of education. If at this stage the confusion is not addressed it becomes the starting point of repeated failure to understand.

The inconsistencies in direction in Maths create confusion. For example, in the two digit numbers such as twenty-two, thirty-six, seventy-five (22, 36, 75,); the numeral are written in the same order as the words. That is, one says thirty-six and writes 3 and 6. However, in the 'teen' numbers like thirteen, fourteen, sixteen (13, 14, 16) one says six-teen and writes 1 and 6 not 6 and 1 (as is the order of the spoken words).

In whole numbers the sequence of words from left to right of the decimal point is units, tens, hundreds, thousands. For decimals, the sequence from right to left of the decimal point is tenths, hundredths, thousandths.

Another classic directional inconsistency is with conveying the time. We say 'twenty to six' and write 5: 40 (six –forty), we say 'twenty past five' and write 5:20 and we also say 'five ten' and write 5:10.

We do subtraction and addition sums right to left

$$\begin{array}{r} 256 \\ +\ 127 \\ \hline \leftarrow \end{array}$$

but do division left to right 3) 693 $\rightarrow$

The six linguistic elements of mathematics that must be methodically taught are symbols, concepts, vocabulary, syntax, voice and translation. Maths has its own terminology. For example ,algebra, logarithm and geometry are Maths words. Maths also shares words with other activities, so 'take away' relates to food (food that is taken away to be eaten) as well as subtraction and words like 'borrowing' (subtraction) and 'carrying' (addition). In numeracy, there is a range of words used to imply the same Maths operation, so we could use add more and plus, to mean add. However, the word 'more' is also used when subtraction has to be carried out as in 'Ella has two more rings than Mina. Ella has six rings, how many rings does Mina have?' Maths requires sequencing abilities. For example, the skill to count on, or back, in twos or threes; or the complex sequence of the steps in the long division procedure. This difficulty can be linked with language problems in questions such as 'Take 12 away from 39' which presents the numbers in the reverse sequence for computation to '39 minus 12' which presents the numbers in the order in which the subtraction is computed. You also need to have good short-term and long term memory to carry out a Maths procedure.

Sharma (1990, p 24) suggests that prerequisite Math skills the student must be able to carry out are to:

- follow sequential directions
- understand and apply classification systems (recognize the value of shapes, quantity, space and change)
- order, organize, and sequence
- have command of spatial orientation and spatial organization (Spatial orientation is our ability to maintain our body orientation and/or posture in relation to the surrounding physical space at rest and during motion) and spatial organization (Spatial organization refers to the arrangement of physical and human objects on the Earth's surface. For example, one's house can be thought of as a point, connected by roads (which are lines)
- understand and employ estimation
- visually cluster objects
- recognize and extend patterns
- visualize or picture

- think deductively (involves conclusion drawn from general principles)
- think inductively (inductive reasoning involves moving from a set of specific facts to broader generalizations and theories)

Difficulties in Maths

The predicament is that difficulty with Maths for itself is extremely common. However, not all children who present low Maths understanding and have poor Maths performance have dyscalculia. Maths underachievement can include a range of emotional and environmental causes, like-lack of motivation or interest in learning mathematics, lack of attention, Maths anxiety, poor systematic Maths instructions and/or school absenteeism for example due to illness.

Four different forms of difficulties in mathematics that have been broadly identified are Acalculia, Dyscalculia, general difficulties in mathematics and Pseudo-dyscalculia. The attributes that differentiate dyscalculia and general difficulties in mathematics and pseudo-dyscalculia are that dyscalculia is a fundamental difficulty with classic concepts of number, time and space.

Dyscalculia is a specific learning difficulty in mathematics as a result of impairment to particular parts of the brain involved in mathematical cognition (Kosc, 1974).

In Acalculia, the student demonstrates a total inability to carry out any mathematical tasks. The total inability to count usually indicates brain damage. A child with 'general learning difficulties in mathematics' displays general problems with all learning, not only with mathematics.

'Pseudo-dyscalculia' is a significant and extensive group in which learning difficulties arise from emotional blockings. Children with pseudo-dyscalculia have the cognitive capacity to be successful in mathematics, notwithstanding their difficulties due to repeated past failures. These failures create deterrents for the child who slowly and steadily avoids all Maths activities (Adler, 2001). 'Math anxiety' is the term given to the feeling of tension and fear that some children (and adults) suffer. It is specifically associated with mathematical activity (Ashcraft, 2002). There is very little research on the overlap between Math anxiety and dyscalculia. It is a reasonable hypothesis that dyscalculia may increase the chances of having math anxiety. Research carried out by Bevan and Butterworth (2002) based on focus groups of dyscalculic children, endorse this view.

Memory, cognitive development and visual-spatial ability are the main areas that a child's Maths disability can start from. A child might have memory problems that interfere with his ability to retrieve (remember) basic arithmetic facts quickly. Memory problem can affect the retrieval of basic Maths facts. In the higher classes it can influence the child's ability to remember the steps needed to solve word problems and solving Geometric problems. The child may have understood the problem performed in school and may not be able to recall it at home or remember it at home but not be able to perform it during the examinations. For example, identifying signs and their meaning (e.g., $+$, $-$, x, $<$, $=$, $>$, %, ?) and automatically remembering answers to basic arithmetic facts such as $3 + 4 = ?$, $9 \times 9 = ?$, $10 \times 0 = ?$

Impediments in cognitive development act as a detriment in the learning and the act of processing information. Understanding relationships between numbers, solving word problems, understanding number systems and using effective counting methods are directly affected by this delay.

Visual-spatial problems interfere with a student's skill to perform math problems correctly: like aligning numerals in columns for calculation problems with place value, trouble deciphering maps and understanding geometry.

Many characteristics of speaking, listening, reading, writing, and arithmetic are common and the same functions of the brain are used to process the information. Consequently, it can be anticipated that children can have a learning disability in more than one area. Some of the indicators of dyscalculia are similar to the indicators of dyslexia (Nation, *et al* 1999). For example, a dyslexic child with a 'visual discrimination problem' would have problems in accurately identifying symbols, gain information from pictures, charts, or graphs. The same problems would affect his Maths skills and reading skills. A child who has difficulties coping with reading 'words' will face a similar problem reading 'word problems'.

Likewise, there is also overlap between dyspraxia and dyscalculia.

In addition while describing manifestations of dyscalculia may be necessary to state that some children (especially those with high IQs) may show signs only Std 8 onwards as that is when they cannot cope up with more difficult Math concepts in algebra and geometry. These children may not have problems with simple arithmetic in lower class standards.

Disorder in Maths

Maths is a subject which involves many skills and therefore disabilities in this area are not simple to categorise. There are various types of Dyscalculia that have been identified. These are tracked down keeping in mind the skill areas of Maths–visual processing, sequencing, language development, generalization–using Maths learned, estimation and short/long term memory–auditory and visual. Kosc (1974), a Czech neuro-psychologist, identified six different types of dyscalculia.

Difficulties that children with dyscalculia may encounter in mainstream school are based upon the skill areas of Maths which are identified as:

1. Visual Processing: (pattern recognition) Visual processing problems often result in difficulties in learning and applying tables, sign confusion, copying and place value.

2. Sequencing: (counting procedures) Sequencing affects rote-learning such as tables and counting forwards and backwards. Signs of these difficulties become more perceptible since the initiation of the numeracy activities that emphasizes mental agility.

3. Language development: The ability to master the language of Maths has a direct relation on choosing appropriate operations to solve Maths problems. The child must be trained to understand and use the six linguistic elements of mathematics-symbols, concepts, vocabulary, syntax, voice and translation correctly.

4. Transferring knowledge and concepts: (applying maths that is learned) If the learner is unable to make generalisations then the load on the memory is increased and difficulties with applying Maths will also increase.

5. Estimation: If a student cannot make a conjecture of the final answer then she has no measure to judge whether the answer is correct. This often occurs when using calculators.

6. Memory: Auditory, visual, short and/ or long term memory deficits result not only in failure to recall number facts but failure to remember instructions given, leading to inability to start the work set.

Thus, these are the problems the child will have which are directly (Adler, 2000) related to the Maths class:

- Symbols, often numeric ones, are written either backwards or in a rotated position.
- Digits that are similar in appearance, such as 6 and 9 or 3 and 8, are confused with each other.

- Failure to take proper note of the distance between digits, so that the numbers 8 and 12 when appearing in succession, for example, are read as 812
- Difficulties in recognizing and making use of the symbols for the four basic types of arithmetic operations
- Problems in understanding maps
- Problems in taking note of objects or symbols when these appear, not singly, but together with other objects or symbols
- Problems in copying numbers, digits or geometric drawings or figures or in reproducing them from memory
- Problems in understanding matters of weight, direction, space or time
- Failure to write down or to read off the correct value of a number that consists of two or more digits
- Problems in understanding the meaning of the symbols for the four basic types of arithmetic operations, such as failure to recall what is the use of a minus-sign
- Problems in shifting from one type of arithmetic operation to another
- Problems in understanding differences in size between different numbers, such as in realizing or remembering that 93 is 4 more than 89
- Problems in grasping the position of a number relative to other numbers, such as in being able to say what number immediately precedes or immediately follows 19
- Having a 'bad memory' for numeric facts
- Having difficulties in carrying out computations in one's head
- Problems in associating words with visual symbols or vice versa, or in reciting the names of things
- Inability to discover a satisfactory way of solving a particular problem
- Problems in shifting from a concrete to an abstract level (in children 10-11 yrs. old or older)
- Problems in remembering what steps to follow in carrying out particular arithmetic or mathematical calculations

- Difficulties in understanding, and in answering either orally or in writing, problems presented to one in either verbal or visual terms
- Problems in carrying out practical, everyday tasks
- Problems in dealing with geometrical figures
- Problems in judging what can be regarded as reasonable
- Problems in planning generally or in following a correct strategy in solving a mathematical problem
- Difficulties in maintaining the overall picture of a given problem, getting lost in details. Problems in dealing with various mathematical units

Kosc (1974), a Czech neuro-psychologist, identified different types of dyscalculia.

1. Verbal dyscalculia: Difficulty in verbal use of Maths symbols and terms; remembering terms and names
2. Practognistic dyscalculia: Inability to recognize distinguishing features or to make comparisons of objects that vary on some dimensions for example, size
3. Lexical dyscalculia: Difficulty reading digits, symbols or multi-digit numbers
4. Graphical dyscalculia: Difficulty writing numbers or symbols
5. Ideological dyscalculia: Difficulty comprehending Maths ideas and making mental computation
6. Operational dyscalculia: Difficulty completing basic operations of addition, subtraction, multiplications and so on

The three sub-types:-

1. Quantitative dyscalculia: This occurs due to weakness in the skills of counting and calculating
2. Qualitative dyscalculia: This is an outcome of difficulties in understanding instructions and/or the failure to learn the skills required for a Maths procedure. For example, when a student has not mastered the prerequisite skill of Maths like

memorisation of number facts, he will face problems with sums involving addition, subtraction, multiplication and division.

3. Intermediate dyscalculia involves the inability to work with symbols or numbers

Etiology

The prevalence of developmental dyscalculia is 6-8% within school children and is as common in girls as in boys. Ability in mathematics is widely seen as an indication for cleverness, and disability in mathematics in school is seen as a marker for low intelligence.

Genetic, neurobiological and epidemiologic evidence indicates that dyscalculia, like other learning disabilities, is a brain-based disorder. However, poor teaching and environmental deprivation have also been linked with the causes of dyscalculia. Due to the reason that the neural network of both hemispheres comprises the substrate of normal arithmetic skills, dyscalculia can result from dysfunction of either hemisphere. Rourke (1993) reports that there are two subtypes of mathematical disabilities: a verbal type, associated with left hemisphere impairment, and a spatial type, associated with right hemisphere impairment.

Dyscalculia can occur as a consequence of pre-maturity and low birth-weight and is frequently encountered in a variety of neurological disorders, such as attention-deficit hyperactivity disorder (ADHD), developmental language disorder, epilepsy, and fragile X syndrome (Shalev, 2004).

Diagnosis and Assessment

Dyscalculia has been identified in a similar fashion like the other specific learning disorders. That is, the diagnosis is made when the individual's achievement or ability in Maths is significantly below that expected for that age, schooling, and level of intelligence.

Even though there are many readymade tests, the most effective method for assessment of Maths deficits is through an informal teacher-testing method. These must be prepared carefully to enable the teacher to analyse the errors and know exactly where the child has a problem and is thus going wrong. These tests are useful because they are specific, practical and easy to implement.

Remedial Strategies

Effective teaching of Maths skills must initiate with the conviction that it is vital for the student to experience success. It has been noted that immediate and continuous successes in Maths for students, is basic for Maths instruction. Additionally when fear sets in, the child is usually not willing to learn and tries to learn the methods in a rote fashion without understanding.

There is a common misconception; since this problem is caused in the brain there can be no remediation; it is a status quo. Research over the last approximately 30 years has revealed that the brain is 'plastic', i.e. it is modified by experience. This implies that the brain is flexible, it compensates for obstacles by adapting and adjusting (Brain briefing, 2000). Effective and continual training programs in reading can result in significant improvement in that particular skill. Researchers in dyslexia has shown that stimulating activities in particular areas of the brain cause growth of neural connections in those active area (Hempenstall, 2006). They suggest that the phrase 'practice makes permanent' holds true. Practicing prolific reading strategies. Practicing productive reading strategies.

These findings are established by brain research which suggests that that the brain never stops changing and adjusting. In the case of Maths, we do not know yet whether the same type of plasticity is present in the brain, but researchers are actively working on this question.

Most up-to-date research proposes that it is very important to ascertain dyscalculia early in children. Even though a complete diagnosis cannot be made until the child is in the 5th-6th standard, nevertheless, it would be extremely advantageous for the child's needs that an early identification is made. This can help understand the particular form of mathematical difficulties the child suffers from, and in turn help form the remediation strategy. There are many programs designed for children with difficulties in mathematics. However, these studies include children who have difficulties in mathematics for all sorts of reasons, not just those with dyscalculia.

We do know that to obtain mathematical understanding children require undertaking their early learning in a multi-sensory mode. They must have repeated practice to reinforce their knowledge in certain areas, such as bonds of ten, achieve automaticity. Understandably, achieving automaticity is more complex and difficult for pupils with a learning difficulty as some of them experience memory deficiency. Moreover, they are usually slow workers and to top it they need more practice than their peers. This makes the situation distressing as they have more workload and they have extra work.

Dyscalculic learners lack an innate grasp of numbers and have problems learning number facts and procedures by the typical and normal technique of teaching. Moreover, due to their inherent difficulties they are never sure that the answer they have arrived at is correct. The self-esteem and confidence of the dyscalculic child should be augmented. The milestone concepts for learning mathematics are: understanding number, place value, fractions, integers, spatial sense and variability. Usually the child's difficulties in mathematics originate from some dysfunction in one of these milestone concepts. Instruction in these areas should be systematically dealt with (Sharma, 2003).

A clear-cut method of understanding and formulating a remedial program suited for the individual child is as follows:

- Help developing the prerequisite skills for mathematics learning
- Facilitate the learning of the missing arithmetic concepts
- Assist the link up of these to their current mathematical needs
- Repetition and practice (automatizing arithmetic facts, daily testing)

Sharma also suggests that remedial should be set to:

- Develop the prerequisite skills in Maths
- Learning Maths facts verbally and off pat
- Visualizing problems and information
- Procedures and estimation should be verbalized and then put in writing
- Counting forward beginning with a given number; for example, begin with 25 and count forward by 1's, 2's, 3's, 10's and so on (Worksheet –Counting forwards and backwards)
- Similarly, counting backwards beginning with a given number; for example begin with 7 and count backward, by 1's, 2's, 5's, and 10's
- Showing patterns of number facts like 1+0 = 0, 2+0=0 involving repeated addition of one (one times table) ... 1, 2, 3, 4, 5, 6, 7, repeated addition of five (five times table) 5, 10, 15, 20, 25, 30, 35 and (for example see the worksheet on Learn addition facts one at a time.)

There are practical methods and instructional designs that can be incorporated into the classroom to help a child with dyscalculia. Experts suggest strategies like the one listed below to help a student who has dyscalculia. This list has suggestions for improving reading skills, improving mathematical problem solving skills, and general instructions.

General Instructional Design

- Supplement missing or incomplete notes
- Break up large sections of text with page breaks and bullet points
- Separate multi-step problems into small, manageable steps
- Use colored felt-tip markers to highlight different parts of a question
- Put up large wall posters to remind students of various basic concepts that cannot be easily recalled in short-term memory
- Use system cards to aid in memorisation
- Provide flow diagrams to clarify procedures
- Provide mind map diagrams to help with the development of a long-term project
- Practice estimating as a way to begin solving math problems
- Move through a lesson at the student's own pace so that he does not become bogged down by the material
- Teach skills in organisation, studying, and time management
- Focus on revision prior to an examination

This list is not a comprehensive one containing all the methods in which to accommodate a dyscalculic student. However, using these approaches in Maths facilitates the learning of all students, regardless of whether or not they have been ascertained as having a Maths learning disorder.

Dyspraxia

If you were asked to describe a child with dyspraxia you would get different answers from the child's physiotherapist, teachers, parent, friends and a speech therapist. The person who interacted with him first, his parents say he is hyperactive, impulsive or a day dreamer. He was very good at learning the 'by-heart stuff' and his manners were of a mature child. A loner, forgetful, unable to make friends with children in his class, disinclined towards sports and games is how his teachers describe him. His friends say he is clumsy, while playing with the ball he cannot catch nor kick properly...he makes the team lose. The speech therapist says he has a sequencing problem with sounds and words and the physiotherapist says he has a motor problem not linked with any medical conditions. This affects his walk, ability to kick and walk on a straight line. When you think of it all seem to be talking about the same child.

Dyspraxia is a difficulty with thinking, planning and carrying out sensory and or motor tasks. The word 'dyspraxia' comes from the word 'dys' meaning difficulty with and the Greek word 'praxis', meaning acting or doing or 'control of movement'. It means poor performance of movements.

The idea of dyspraxia has been discussed in the research literature for almost 100 years. However, it was as late as the 1980's, that individuals with neurological problem with motor · planning were differentiated from amongst the population and dyspraxia was identified as a specific learning disability (Dighe and Kettles, 1996). Nevertheless, there continues to be a lack of agreement concerning both the definition and description of this disorder. Labels used to recognize this learning disability include-Developmental Awkwardness, Sensorimotor Dysfunction, Minimal Brain Dysfunction, Motor Sequencing Disorder, Disorder of Sensory Integration, Clumsy Child Syndrome, Developmental Coordination Disorder and most recently Specific Developmental Disorder of Motor Function.

The recent definition of Developmental dyspraxia is: 'delay or disorder of the planning and/or execution of complex movements... Associated with this may be problems of language, perception and thought' (Colley, 2000, p.10).

Learning disabilities caused as a result of Dyspraxia has not been researched on extensively. The most important reasons for that are because of its inherent problems, which are that it is difficult to detect and diagnose. Dyspraxia may also overlap with other Special Educational Needs, for example, Dyslexia, Attention Deficit Hyperactivity Disorder and Aspergers Syndrome making it even more difficult to pin-point. Researchers accept that it is a neurological disorder with a hereditary element. Yet, brain imaging researches have not established a correlation between dyspraxia and specific areas of the brain or differences in brain development.

However, we do know that dyspraxia is a neurologically based developmental disability which is present from birth. Dyspraxia is understood to be an immaturity of parts of the motor cortex (area of the brain) that prevents messages from being properly transmitted to the body. Dyspraxia does not have an influence on intelligence. It is important to remember that children with dyspraxia have average or above average intelligence. Further, like other speech and language difficulties, verbal dyspraxia is not a static condition. It has been suggested that there can and will be adjustment and alteration over a period.

It is a motor planning disorder, not a muscular deficit. A child knows what they want their body to perform but cannot get their body to carry it out. Children with this disability appear the same as any other child. It is only when a skill is performed that the disability is noticeable. Dyspraxia is a hidden handicap. Dyspraxia can impact on behavior and social skills. Dyspraxia affects up to 10% of the population. It occurs more frequently in males than females (Colley, 2000).

Individuals with dyspraxia may or may not have learning disabilities. The symptoms from these learning disabilities can be similar to those of a person with dyspraxia. Research in this area point out that children with more severe dyspraxia tend to overlap with children who have Attention Deficit Hyperactivity Disorders (ADHD), High-Functioning Autism, Asperger's Syndrome and Tics Disorders which are not learning disabilities. The reason the author has included Dyspraxia in this chapter and book as she is of the opinion that since, though not always, Dyspraxia often co-exists with other learning disabilities, such as dyslexia (difficulty reading, writing and spelling) and dyscalculia (difficulty with mathematics); it would be of assistance to have information on this particular subject.

The child with dyspraxia may have a combination of several problems in varying degrees –

- Poor co-ordination and listening skills
- Poor visual and auditory perception
- Poor sequencing in visual-motor and auditory-verbal tasks
- Lack of spatial and directional awareness
- Poor perception of self within the environment
- Poor memory and short attention span, and are especially slow in recalling information in stressful situations
- Poor balance
- Poor fine and gross motor co-ordination. Have problems that include complex motor skills involving sequences of movements and their gross motor skills are late in developing. Have difficulty in learning and are 'awkward' with fine motor skills
- Poor posture
- Difficulty with throwing and catching a ball
- Poor awareness of body position in space
- Poor sense of direction

- Difficulty hopping, skipping or riding a bike
- Sensitive to touch
- Confused about which hand to use
- Intolerance of having hair or teeth brushed, nails and hair cut
- Slow to learn to dress or feed themselves
- Find some clothes uncomfortable
- Difficulty with reading, writing
- Speech problems–slow to learn to speak and speech may be incoherent
- Poor visual memory and perception
- Poor visual-spatial differentiation and sequencing problems
- Phobias or obsessive behavior and impatient

Dyspraxia may affect any or all areas of development–physical, intellectual, emotional, social, language, and sensory and may impair the normal process of learning, therefore is a learning difficulty. Moreover, it is an inconsistent disorder in which the symptoms may be different in different children. Furthermore, a particular child can experience a set of problems on one day and not on the next day. The typical problems are divided into the following areas.

Areas Affected by Dyspraxia

Movement

Gross and fine motor skills are hard to learn. Performances of these skills are awkward, hesitant and poor.

Language

Verbalization may be immature or even unintelligible in early years. Furthermore, language development may be late.

Perception

Poor understanding of the messages that the senses convey and difficulty in relating those messages to actions. There is a lack of ability to understand gesture, voice tone and body language, difficulty adjusting to changes and deficits in social judgment and interaction.

Thought

Difficulty is experienced in planning and organizing thoughts. Those with moderate learning difficulties have such problems to a greater extent.

Signs to recognize a child with dyspraxia

The pre-school child

- Is late in reaching milestones for example rolling over, sitting, standing, walking, and speaking
- May not be able to run, hop, jump, or catch or kick a ball although children their age can
- Has difficulty in walking up and down stairs
- Poor at dressing
- Slow and hesitant in most actions
- Appears not to be able to learn anything instinctively but must be taught skills
- Falls over frequently
- Poor pencil grip
- Cannot do jigsaws or shape sorting games
- Artwork is very immature
- Often anxious and easily distracted

The school age child

- Probably has all the difficulties experienced by the pre-school child with dyspraxia, with little or no improvement
- Avoids physical education and games
- Does badly in class but significantly better on a one-to-one basis

- Reacts to all stimuli without discrimination and attention span is poor
- May have trouble with maths and writing structured stories
- Experiences great difficulty in copying from the blackboard
- Writes laboriously and immaturely
- Unable to remember and /or follow instructions
- Is generally poorly organised

Types of Dyspraxia

To reiterate, dyspraxia is not a muscle condition. To put it simply, the brain is sending a message to the muscle but the message is getting scrambled hence the muscle is doing something different or is doing it too slowly. That is because even though the brain is okay and the muscle is okay the message is not being translated properly.

Dyspraxia is divided into two types:

1. **Ideational dyspraxia** – Difficulty with planning a sequence of coordinated movements.
2. **Ideo-motor dyspraxia** – Difficulty with executing a plan, even though it is known
   Dyspraxia affects speech and language, handwriting and drawing, body movements and physical play.

   - With speech and language, children have difficulty with controlling speech organs, making sounds, forming words, and controlling their breathing
   - With handwriting and drawing they have problems learning the basic movement patterns of images, a writing speed, and how to properly hold a writing instrument- like pencil or pen
   - With body movements, children often struggle with timing, balance; they have difficulty with merging movements into a sequence and remembering the next movement in a sequence

- With physical play, children are inclined to have problems with ball movements

Dyspraxia further falls into three categories: Oral, Verbal and Motor. A child with dyspraxia can have one or a combination of all three types of dyspraxia and in varying degrees of severity.

Oral dyspraxia is a difficulty with planning and executing non-speech sounds and breathing patterns such as blowing, sucking and/or experiencing difficulty in putting their tongue up to the roof of their mouth. This may affect speech and/or swallowing skills. Given that the child with Oral Dyspraxia experiences problems with the mouth movement he may dribble a lot, have difficulty licking an ice-cream and may have a preference for either soft or hard textured foods.

Verbal dyspraxia is a speech disorder that affects the programming, sequencing and initiating of movements required to make speech sounds. They do not have control on their speech muscles. Have difficulty making purposeful movement of the tongue and lips as they attempt to make a sound and lucid speech. As they have problems making a speech sound they often cannot make the same sound again. They are inclined to simplifying words. Some put forward highly unintelligible speech and adopt a complex gesture system to aid communication skills (Boon, 2001).

Motor dyspraxia is a difficulty in planning, sequencing and then executing the correct movement to perform age appropriate skills in a smooth and coordinated manner at will or on command. Lack of motor control can manifest in social rejection, as this child is clumsy and constantly getting in the way, colliding into people and objects. The child is generally oblivious of the position in space his body encompasses. Besides social isolation, the child's motor disabilities and spatial misconceptions put him at a risk for personal injury. They do not show a consistent performance nor do they display age appropriate skills. They are awkward at generalizing learnt skills and weak at timing and rhythm. This problem is further divided into poor gross motor or poor fine motor skills.

Poor gross motor skills can affect their performance during PT (Physical Training) and in the dance class. Throwing, catching and kicking a ball can be awkward and tough. Running and even walking can appear ungainly as balance and gross motor skills are not automatic.

Fine motor skills affect the child's ability to write, draw etc. The drawing and artwork of a dyspraxic person may well appear unsophisticated, messy or undeveloped. Painting with a fine brush is likely to take more concentrated effort than for other students. Similarly tasks such as shading in or labelling diagrams are poorly executed. Students may have difficulty using scissors.

Causes of Dyspraxia

For most children there is no known cause, although it is thought to be an immaturity of neuron development in the brain rather than brain damage. Dyspraxic children have no clinical neurological abnormality to explain their condition, but the source of dyspraxic difficulties is thought to be within immature neuronal development. Such immaturity within left hemispheric development of the brain may be particularly implicated.

Possible factors may include:

1. Pre-natal trauma
2. Environmental deprivation
3. Febrile illness in the early years
4. Neurological Trauma
5. Genetic factors

6. Neurological immaturity
7. Unestablished cerebral dominance

How to Help

Work with the dyspraxic child's strengths, as these children are usually very creative, sensitive and caring. They develop their own way of doing things, which should be encouraged. Aim to be patient with them and do not keep interrupting or completing a sentence for them. Let them learn to do things at their own speed. Stay away from nagging and correcting as this can make the child tense and angry. Try to keep to routines as children with dyspraxia are sensitive and tend to panic easily and respond badly to sudden changes in routine. They are not happy working outside their comfort zone and are scared easily.

A child with verbal difficulty needs specialist help from speech therapists and often physiotherapists and occupational therapists as well. They have to be trained deliberately about how the lips and tongue works to form all the different sounds and words.

A child with eye-tracking difficulties who has problems in copying from the blackboard or a book can gain from help from a developmental optometrist. A developmental optometrist will identify problems with control over eye muscles and eye tracking difficulties, and suggest exercises to help.

Activity ideas to use at home to help skills development

Multi-sensory teaching should be used whenever possible.

Gross motor–These gross movements come from large muscle groups and whole body movement such functions as walking, kicking, sitting upright, lifting, and throwing a ball.

Do lots of activities involving hand, eye and body coordination.

These should include:

- catching and throwing
- kicking
- crawling through obstacle courses
- climbing
- standing on wobble boards
- space hopper- a large ball to sit and bounce on
- throwing and catching: balloons, bubbles large foam balls (textured surface) rings, beanbags, scarves (thin floating material)

Fine motor–Fine motor skills involve the small muscles of the body and can be defined as coordination of small muscle movements which occur in the fingers, usually in coordination with the eyes, like when writing or fastening buttons.

- strengthening finger muscles
- finger games
- puppets finger
- painting
- plasticine

Finger sensitivity: blindfold games; feeling textures with eyes closed like bubble wrap, sand paper, wool

Handwriting: finger writing in sand, other textured surfaces pencil mazes dot-to-dot books tracing, stencils pencil grips, fat pencils (large size) triangular pens/pencils

Other activities: buttoning, lacing, bead threading, lace threading, cards, pattern copying

Reading: activities to improve visual tracking (eye movements left to right for reading) left to right pencil games; for example take bee to the flower (drawn on paper) rolling ball left to right

Learning the names of body parts with the help of:

- Puzzles on body parts
- 'Twister' game and
- 'Simon Says' games

Timely identification can play a significant role in helping the child with dyspraxia. It is important to set up a pattern of consistent remedial measures in which parents, therapists and teachers can work together. The longer the child with dyspraxia goes without being identified, the greater the experience of failure and thus frustration sets in. The more often they are criticised and scolded, the poorer their self esteem and self confidence becomes. It is important to remember that dyspraxia is not a disease and thus there is no cure for it. The main aim of treatment is to help the child circumnavigate his difficulties, to learn and to achieve his goals.

CHAPTER 6

SOCIAL FACTORS

In this chapter I explore the social factors that affect children with learning disabilities. Compared with their schoolmates without developmental problems, these children have lower self-esteem, have more depression and anxiety, and play truant more often. This adds strain on the relations at home and school. This chapter stresses on the need for extra emotional support and help, a learning disabled child requires in everyday life

A familiar learning characteristic of children with learning disabilities is that they have difficulty with the scholastic subjects in school. In addition to academic problems children with learning disabilities frequently have difficulty with emotional and social behaviors that are more debilitating than the academic problems like maths, reading and writing. These often add to a heavy psychological burden. For many, feelings of frustration, anger, sadness, or shame can lead to psychological difficulties such as low self-esteem, anxiety or depression. Occasionally, occurrences of behavioral problems such as substance abuse or juvenile delinquency are seen in children with learning disability.

Often individuals with learning disabilities will display one or more of the following characteristics:

- Limited ability to abstract and generalise
- Limited social skills
- Inappropriate or immature personal behavior
- Limited attention span and poor retention ability
- Decreased motivation
- Poor self-concept
- Low self-esteem
- General clumsiness
- Lack of coordination and of gross and fine motor skills
- Emotional disturbance

Mainstreaming

In the early eighties, conceptual shifts in ways of thinking about children with learning disability began to emerge, suggesting that separating and excluding children from their natural school environment did not always have positive consequences (Colfer, Farrelly, Limerick, Grealy and Smyth, 2000). The integration of children with learning disability into mainstream schools is an important social and educational issue.

The UNESCO Salamanca Statement (1994) states that:

> 'Inclusion and participation are essential to human dignity and exercise of human rights' ... 'The fundamental principle of the inclusive school is that all children should learn together, wherever possible, regardless of any difficulties or differences they may have.' (p.18)

There was a paradigm shift from integrated education to inclusive education, laying stress on a broadened education service for the child with disabilities. The term integration and terms such as mainstreaming and inclusive have been used concurrently. However, the term inclusive education is different from integration:

> *'In integration learners with disabilities are placed in a regular school without making any changes in the school to accommodate and support the diverse needs. Inclusive education, by comparisons seeks to adapt systems and structures to meet the needs of all learners. Moving from integration to inclusion requires changes/adaptations at various levels including to the curriculum, attitudes, values, language etc. These adaptations are made by fully involving the learners in the process. ...Inclusion is based on a social model of disability that views disability as a socially created problem and management of problem requires social action in the form of environmental modifications necessary for the full participation of persons with disabilities in every sphere of life.'*

(Scheme of Integrated Education for the Disabled Children (IEDC) India, 1986: section, 3.1; updated in 1992)

However, the question 'is mainstreaming good for the child with learning disability?' needs to be answered. Investigations (IEDC, 1986; Clarks, Dyson and Milward, 1995; Frederickson and Cline, 2002) show that inclusive education results in improved social development and academic outcomes for all learners. It leads to the development of social skills and better social interactions because learners are exposed to a natural environment in which they have to interact with other learners, each one having unique characteristics, interests and abilities.

Nevertheless, inclusive outcomes appear to be problematic for students with learning disability (Cook, 2001). It is conventionally believed that the children with learning disability benefit largely from inclusion due to the lack of meaningful difference between them and their non-disabled peers (Wang, Reynolds and Walberb, 1988). However, Cook (2001) suggests students with learning disability are at greater risk for receiving inappropriate educational interactions for different reasons.

The first reason is that children with learning disability do not reveal obvious signs of their disabilities, like for example children who are physically challenged. Therefore, they are expected to attain model performance and behavior standards. Thus, when a student with learning disability behaves typically or falls below the level of academic performance of an average student in class, they are looked on as an indifferent student. Teachers have brief and token interactions with children they perceive as indifferent students, suggests Cook (2001; Silberman, 1971; Good and Brophy, 1972). In a typical Indian class of fifty children, children with learning disability, fall outside the teacher's tolerance level (cf. Cook, 2001).

Secondly, students with learning disability are not well accepted by their non-disabled peers (Cook and Semmel, 1999). They are rejected precisely because they are perceived to be 'just like everyone else', yet their academic achievements and classroom behavior suggests they are disparate.

Thirdly, the reason children with learning disability are especially vulnerable, particularly in the Indian milieu, is that teachers do not know how to deal with these children (cf. Edwards, 1994). There is a visible lack of teacher training in the field of learning disabilities. Even though, in India, the Persons with Disabilities (Equal Opportunities, Protection of Rights and Full Participation) Act, 1995 (PWD Act, 1995) suggests that schemes will be provided for the programme of training with regard to inclusive education to special teachers, general teachers and educational administrators, this is only on paper. There are many provisions made for children with learning disorder, however, a few are actually implemented.

Edwards (1994) suggests that the damage by inadequate or incompetent teaching is not irreversible nor are difficult or disruptive behavior patterns, a permanent feature of the child with learning disability. As an essential part of preparation for adult life, students with learning disability should also be offered programmes with an emphasis on life skills.

Social skills problems can be viewed as errors in learning; therefore, the appropriate skills need to be taught directly and actively. If students are expected to learn appropriate social skills their learning environment must be structured to enable them to practice pro-social skills (Algozzine, Ruhl and Ramsey, 1991). Activities that foster social and personal development, such as physical education, sports, leisure activities, arts and crafts, should also be emphasized. Success heals many wounds and strengthens self-image, suggests Edwards (1994) and sometimes even a single incident of positive feedback can alter a child's self-concept (Riddick, 1996).

Studies show that social and emotional skills are the most consistent indicators of success for students with learning disability, even more so than academic factors. The way children can cope with stress, whether they blame themselves for their failure or handle it productively, has a great impact on their learning. This in turn affects their self-esteem and self-concept (Fontana, 1995; Elbaum and Vaughn, 1999). The stress a child with learning disability undergoes (Table 2) considerably more than his/her peers. Johnson (2005) suggests that about 30% of children with learning disability have behavioral and emotional problems. Additionally, she suggests that those adolescents with learning disability had high rates of depression and alarming rates of suicide.

Table 1: Effects of Stress on the Child with Learning Disability

Behavior	Withdrawal, avoidance and absenteeism, doing nothing and apathy, 'taking out feeling' on others, tendency to blame others, hostility, unpredictable and uncharacteristic behavior.
Thinking	Rigidity, making decisions and setting priorities.
Cognition	Difficulty in concentration and distractibility increases, forgetfulness and rate of error increases, decreased power of observation, reduction in memory span.
Emotion	Panic, the feeling of worthlessness, frustration, lowered self-esteem, anger, irritability, anxiety, emotional outbursts increase, depression.
Physical demeanor	Exhaustion can manifest in physical pains like headaches and stomach aches, speech problems like stammering, stuttering, hesitancy and disturbed sleep pattern.

(compiled from Fontana, 1995; Miles and Varma, 1995; Ott, 1997; Cornwall, 1999)

Investigators have stressed the need for management of high anxiety and low self-esteem in children with learning disability (Ramaa, 2000). This area is important to understand because the emotional stability of dyslexic children is a pre-requisite which underlines teaching and research (Edwards, 1994). Research suggests that children with learning disabilities show:

• Higher incidence of depression
• Higher levels of anxiety

- Poor self esteem
- Poor achievement motivation
- Higher rates of suicidal tendencies
- Increased feelings of frustration and isolation

Initially, researchers focused on academic and cognitive characteristics of an individual with learning disability; however, more recently there has emerged an increased interest in their social abilities (Edwards, 1994; Elbaum and Vaughn, 1999).

The development of psychosocial skills is required to deal with the demands and challenges of everyday life. Life skills education is aimed at facilitating psychosocial skills and includes the application of life skills in the context of situations where children and adolescents need to be empowered. This enhances the children's mental well-being, self esteem, self worth and capabilities which should be the objectives of good education. This is something that is overlooked in the Indian school setting. The number of tuition classes and special coaching classes attest this. In India, the primary concern is to see that the students pass their board examinations. The children's mental health is sadly overlooked and a life skills capacity building agenda is often ignored in the Indian school settings. When a student has been assessed with a learning disability, great emphasis is put on her academic inabilities and the child is coached to overcome them. There is rarely any importance given to the child's psychosocial competence.

Understanding the Reasons for the Psychological and Emotional Problems

Understanding the perceptible reasons for the psychological and emotional problems a child with learning disabilities face would enable us to effectively support them. Considering the repeated failure in their school life with academics, it is not surprising that a learning disabled child would have psychological difficulties. They have to continually and regularly fight with the educational system with their needs being ignored or misunderstood.

Often a child with learning disabilities who has not been diagnosed correctly has to endure the emotional burden of not getting proper help and treatment. It is not unusual for a child who is described as a quiet and well-behaved in school to be bad tempered and sometimes violent at home. Parents and siblings see a totally different child than the teachers and school friends do. The hard work and energy put in to perform in school takes it's toll and when the child returns home he/she has run out of energy, and the bad temper and violent mood swings occur. This adds extra strain on the relations at home.

Moreover the child hardly ever receives positive feed back and often labelled as a 'shirker' 'slow' 'lazy' and or 'dumb'. The child is rarely given an opportunity to present his talents and usually made to work on his worst subjects where he experiences repeated failures.

Such negative feeling only promotes negative self-image, low self-esteem and low self-confidence. Considering that the child has average to above average intelligence and divergent thinking, the signs of low self-esteem in a learning disabled child are often masked as he/she is clever enough to do so.

Self-defeating Masked Strategies

- **Clowning**–the child becomes the class joker to hide pressure experienced in the class, or to hide the lack of confidence and also to try to attract attention and be liked as well as to make an effort to acquire friends
- **Quitting**–when the assignment becomes too hard and frustrating

- **Avoiding**–and doing it half heartedly. Both are done to avoid the fear of failing... 'I did not try hard enough and that is why I did not do well'
- **Aggressiveness**–to counteract the feeling of vulnerability
- **Impulsiveness**–to get over the task as quickly as possible

Occasional wasteful stratagems, such as the ones mentioned above, are not a cause for concern. However, when they become consistent and regular way the child approaches daily studies then parents need to look into the feelings behind this kind of behavior and help. For the reason that, this kind of behavior pattern not only interfere with learning but also affect the child's mental health and his ability to enjoy life.

Some children with learning difficulties may become either anxious as a consequence of ongoing academic or non-academic struggles related to their learning difficulties. A child who is anxious may seem worried most of the time. He may well act nervous in certain settings, such as in crowded places, at school or when expected to perform. He may fear being separated from home or his parents and may experience separation anxiety disorder. Children with learning disabilities may experience somatic complaints, such as headaches and stomach aches which are a common symptom of anxiety at all ages.

Fear of Failure

The pressure on children with learning disabilities is often of an understated kind. Many children with learning disabilities feel they are letting down their parents and family whenever they fail. They perceive the frustration their parents experience when their parents are trying to teach them or understand their problem. This in turn frustrates them and makes them anxious. Moreover, no matter how hard they try they cannot keep up with their non-disabled classmates. This too creates stress and anxiety. It makes them lose their self-respect. Stress in turn creates failure and the learning disabled child is caught in a never ending whirlpool.

Fear of being 'Different'

One does not fear being 'different' if one is successful. Nevertheless the child with learning disabilities is different for all the wrong reasons. They either do not read and write like their schoolmates, or they do not spell like them. They cannot throw the ball and kick like the peers. Sometimes they have a poor balance or sometimes they speak differently. Anxiety is one consequence of being different. Children with learning disabilities are unsure and are not certain if they can trust their vision of the world, because they see it differently. Their visual or auditory processing may not be accurate, their thinking or time management may be to a degree chaotic, or they may have trouble reading subtle social cues. Subsequently, many children feel out of control within and try to take control in other aspects of their lives.

Occasionally the methods used to cope with this type of fear makes it worse. Sometimes they think if I am 'different' I might as well be different in a big way. This type of thinking produces oppositional behavior, bullying or being disruptive. They veer into a self-deception mode with the belief that. 'if I deny it, it will disappear'. That is adopting a denial approach in order to manage the pain they would feel if their insecurities were in fact acknowledged. All the above mentioned coping strategies are harmful to their emotional make-up.

Depression

Young people today face significant stresses in their lives. Some stresses are a part of growing up, others are more individual, involving pressures to advance in school and earn a living. Children negotiate these stresses with varying degrees of resilience and mastery. Hendren, Weisen and Orley (1994) suggest that at least 3% of school-aged children suffer from serious mental illnesses such as severe depression, suicidal thoughts, psychosis, serious attention problem or obsessive-compulsive disorder. A study conducted in Mumbai (Kaila, SNDT in Ashar, 2005), which is a part of a global project focusing on the victimisation of children at school suggested that the figure is relatively higher. The study reported that every seventh school going child might have harbored suicidal thoughts on more than three occasions.

Recently in Mumbai four students committed suicide in a period of three days (Ashar, 2005) and all were related to academic failure and stress. According to Dr Dhavale, head of the psychiatry department, Nair Hospital (in Sharma, 2003), parents and teachers need to convince the youth that things may not always go according to their wishes. In such a situation, the person must learn to accept any setback and learn the skills to get over it.

The above is concerned with the research done on all children. Experts believe that a child with learning disabilities is at a greater risk of depression. Research on depression faced by children with learning disabilities has been conducted for nearly 30 years. Children with learning disabilities were believed to be at greater risk of depression than children without learning disabilities. Research suggests that about 5% to 20% of children with learning disabilities experience symptoms of depression. This is much higher than the 3% rate inferred for all children. The child with learning disabilities often has low self-esteem which is a forewarning to depression. Poor school performance, repeated failure and thus low motivation are all linked to low self-esteem. Even a simple act like reading can affect ones self-esteem. When poor readers like the child with dyslexia has to read out aloud in class, it can affect their self-esteem and confidence. Being put in a negative situation from which they cannot escape makes the child become apathetic and demoralised.

What exactly causes depression is not known. However, studies in depression imply that depression possibly involves hereditary, neurological, and environmental components. It is important to understand depression. Depression is not merely a feeling of sadness that one experiences now and then. The signs of depression are listed below. Most or nearly all these symptoms must be experienced persistently over 2-3 weeks to classify the emotional state as depression.

Depression is a condition characterized by:

- Extreme feelings of sadness
- Lack of interest or pleasure in most or all activities
- Significant weight gain or loss
- Sleeping too little or too much
- Restlessness or exhaustion
- Low energy
- Feeling worthless
- Difficult in concentrating
- Thoughts of suicide

Children with learning disabilities may experience depression. However, there is no reason for any child to suffer from depression when effective treatments are available. There are several steps one can take to help them. The most important is to become familiar with the symptoms of depression. If you suspect that the child has a problem, visit a psychiatrist.

Though children with learning disability experience difficulties in academic performance, they are often bright, creative, and talented individuals; their forte may include mechanical aptitude, artistic ability, musical gifts, and athletic prowess (Yosimoto, 2000). However, the student's days are then planned with remedial activities based on their weaknesses rather than their strengths. In the remedial class greater emphasis is laid on the student's weaknesses which continue to adversely impact on their self-esteem. If a child is weak in mathematics or language she usually attends the remedial class in school during the music or art class, thus probably missing a subject she is accomplished in and finds enjoyable!

Researchers and clinicians have emphasized the importance of replenishing areas of strength in building self-confidence. Rutter (1985), in discussing resilient individuals, observed: '... *experience of success in one arena of life led to enhanced self-esteem and a feeling of self-efficacy, enabling them to cope more successfully with the subsequent life challenges and adaptation.'* (p.604)

Being able to display our talents, and to have them valued by important people in our lives, helps us to define our identities around that which we do best. Thus, enrichment classes, like drama, painting, pottery, singing and dancing, can be suitable to enhance the students' talents (Yosimoto, 2000).

One of the most powerful approaches for helping students feel competent is to lessen their fear of failure (Ott, 1997). Besides the parents teachers can play an important role in identifying (but not diagnosing) children who may be depressed. Teachers have a large role to play in this issue. This is because it is the teacher who meets the children on a daily basis. It is the teacher who first encounters the problems a child faces. Effective teachers recognize that if children and adolescents with learning disability are to succeed and become more hopeful in school, their basic needs to belong and feel connected, to be active participants in their own education and to experience the joys of competence and accomplishment must be met.

If the teacher makes learning an enjoyable experience for their pupils they could achieve much better results in the classroom. It would not only enhance motivation to learn but would additionally enhance the children's self-esteem. When children enjoy whatever they are doing, they are going through what Csikszentmihalyi (1990) calls a 'flow experience'. A flow experience is an experiential state that distinguishes an enjoyable moment from the rest of life. Csikszentmihaly (1990) suggests that the feeling is like being carried away by a current, like being in a flow. A teacher who understands the conditions that make children want to learn is in a position to turn classroom activities into flow experiences.

How can parents help:

- Set out very slowly. If you immediately focus on their anxiety, it is going to make the child more anxious.
- Try to create a non-threatening environment
- Physical touch is extremely important for soothing anxiety
- Listen to the child's feelings. Their language problems may make it difficult for them to express their feelings.
- Reward effort, not just 'the outcome'
- Help students set realistic goals for themselves this can alter the cycle of failure. Do not use negative words like stupid, lazy and dumb.
- Recognize and rejoice in his successes be it in athletics, art or mechanics.

- Help them to think better about themselves and deal effectively with their feelings which is a complex task.
- Get professional help

Caring adults must understand the cognitive and affective problems caused by learning disabilities. Then, they must plan strategies that will help the child, like every other child, to find joy and success in academics and personal relationships.

CHAPTER 7

HOW IS LEARNING DISABILITY ASSESSED?

How is Learning Disability Identified?

The first step in solving any problem is realizing there is one. From the time the child is born the mother and other members of the family are constantly keeping track of the child's developmental milestones. Therefore the first persons to notice any obvious delays in their child reaching early milestones would be the family members. During routine checkups the pediatrician monitors and looks out for the minute signs of development. The pediatrician may observe more subtle signs of minor neurological damage, such as a lack of coordination. The parents and the pediatrician are watching for the child to achieve developmental milestones.

The class teacher may be the next to notice a child's persistent difficulties in reading, writing or arithmetic. The child's teacher may be the first to observe that the child's speaking or listening skills are not at the level expected for children of his/her age. The teacher may notice that the child has trouble responding to the questions about a story she has just heard, or following her spoken directives for work done in the class.

The learning problems of children who are quiet and polite in school may go unnoticed. Children with above average intelligence, who manage to maintain passing grades despite their disability, are even less likely to be identified. Children with learning disabilities who have superior intelligence on their own may develop strategies to overcome their problems. These children may not experience school failure but their marks/ grades would be below their potential.

Sometimes it is better to allow a little more time if critical developmental milestones have not occurred by the usual age. That is basically for the brain to mature a bit. However, if a milestone is already long delayed and if there is a history of learning disabilities in the family and /or if there are several delayed skills, the child should be professionally evaluated as soon as possible. The child's pediatrician and /or the school counsellor can be of help in this situation.

Karande, et al (2005) suggests that a pediatrician can enable early detection of learning disability by:

1. Keeping a track of the child's growth and inquiring about the child's school performance during a consultation
2. Guiding the parents for getting their child's psycho-educational assessment done, when learning disability is suspected
3. Counselling the parents and class teacher of a child with learning disability, about the need for remedial education and provisions
4. Monitor the child's academic progress on a long term basis

Diagnosis

Testing and assessment is imperative for children suspected of having a learning disability because:

1. It communicates vital information about the child's suspected disability.

2. If the child meets the criteria, it makes available specific information to enable the special educator to develop an Individual Education Programme (IEP).
3. It is required by the National/State Educational Boards regulations to determine eligibility and grant provisions/ accommodations (see the end of the chapter and Appendix).

For a complete and comprehensive evaluation of a child who is suspected to be learning disabled the corroboration of a multidisciplinary team is availed on. The multidisciplinary team comprises of paediatrician, counsellor, clinical psychologist and special educator (Kulkarni, et al, 2001). Before the diagnosis of learning disability is confirmed the team confers and gives a mutually agreed assessment.

Assessment and testing are complex processes of gathering information in all areas related to a student's suspected disability.

1. Review of educational records
2. Observations
3. Review of students' work
4. Medical, vision, and hearing and audiological examination
5. Developmental and Social History
6. Fine and Gross Motor Evaluation
7. Adaptive Behavior
8. Speech and Language Assessment
9. Intellectual Ability or 'IQ' tests
10. Assessment of Academic Skills
11. Social and Emotional Assessment
12. Behavioral Assessment
13. Psychiatric Evaluation
14. Audiometric and ophthalmic examinations are done to rule out non-correctable hearing and visual deficits. This is done as children with these deficits do not qualify for a diagnosis of learning disability.

The Paediatrician studies the detailed clinical history of the child. The detailed clinical history involves scrutinizing the past and present records of the child. Furthermore, he performs a detailed neurological examination. A thorough physical examination is completed to exclude medical causes. For example, hypothyroidism, chronic lead poisoning; and neurological causes, cerebral palsy and Wilson's disease. It is also performed to identify the possibly behavioral causes; for example, Attention Deficit Hyperactivity Disorder (ADHD), Depression, Conduct Disorder, or Oppositional Defiant Disorder of poor school performance. This information presents a picture of the child over time.

1. Health and developmental history
2. Results of vision and hearing tests
3. Previous schools attended and educational history
4. Group test results and report cards
5. Reports from previous teachers
6. Attendance and discipline records
7. Diversity issues, such as primary language, culture, etc
8. Information from other professionals who have worked privately with the child

The counsellor ruled out the possibility of emotional problems resulting from predicaments like stress at home, abuse, parental separation or death of a loved one. In a few cases emotional problem are the principal reasons for the child's academic underachievement. The counsellor rules out any such possibilities. It is important to remember that apart from learning disability there are other causes for children to under perform, such as, chronic medical illnesses, borderline intelligence ('slow learners'), visual or hearing deficit, isolated ADHD, emotional problems, and poor socio-cultural home environment. However, a history of language delay, or of not attending to the sounds of words (trouble playing rhyming games with words, or confusing words that sound alike), along with a family history, are important warning signs for learning disability in preschool children.

The clinical psychologist conducted the standard test, by the use of, Wechsler Intelligence Scale for Children - Revised (WISC) [Indian adaptation by MC Bhatt], to determine that the child's level of intellectual functioning was average or above average (Global Intelligence Quotient score ≥85) (Karande et al , 2007). This facilitates the exclusion of borderline intellectual functioning and mild mental retardation, which are also causes for poor school performance.

Full Scale IQ Score

A measure of the child's overall/global intellectual functioning (or g) is derived from the composite of subtests administered on the Wechsler. The Full Scale IQ score has been researched for decades, and appears significantly related to academic achievement, occupational level, and educational attainment.

Full Scale IQ scores:

Very Superior +: Over 140

Superior: 120-140

High Average: 110-119

Average: 90 -109

Low average: 80-89

Borderline: 70-79

Intellectually Deficit: < 69

The Special Educator assesses the child's academic achievement by administering standard educational tests for example, Wide Range Achievement Test, Peabody Individual Achievement Test, Woodcock-Johnson Tests of Achievement,

Schonnel Attainment Test, Curriculum Based Test) to assess the child's performance in areas such as reading, spelling, written language, and mathematics.

Reading assessment: Specific reading disabilities are recorded by analyzing the reading performance. These disabilities are generally: reading word by word, omissions, reversals, insertions and guessing at words.

Assessment of spellings: The ability to spell is accepted as a complex and multifaceted process. A competent assessment process can plainly summarize the relevant skills a child has or has not mastered, shows patterns of errors and provide direction for systematic remedial instructions.

Assessment of maths skills: There are a number of Maths assessment kits. Sadly they produce little usable teaching information. However, informal assessment which consists of observation, oral interviews and error analysis can provide sufficient information regarding the child's Maths abilities.

Other areas assessed include handwriting, comprehension and attention. These tests are used for children above six years of age. The assessment report predominantly brings out the level at which the child functions in each area of learning skills and the nature of the disabilities that the child exhibits. Based on this report, an Individual Remedial Programme (IEP) is prepared for each child.

An academic achievement of upto two years below the child's actual school grade placement or chronological age is considered diagnostic of learning disability.

[Please note: Cranial CT/MRI scan, electroencephalogram, and blood tests (e.g., vitamin B12 / folate levels, thyroid hormone levels, and lead levels) are not necessary for diagnosing learning disability (Karande et al , 2007)].

Why a Timely Diagnosis is Important?

At the heart of treatment of learning disability is 'remedial education'. Karande (2008) suggests that presently, learning disability cannot be conclusively diagnosed until the child is about seven to eight years old. However, he continues by explaining that because of the central nervous system's higher plasticity in early years, remedial education should be started as early as possible (Karande, 2008). Experts recommend that when the child is in primary school, that is before the age of ten years remedial treatment should be started to achieve maximum advantage.

It is presently understood that the brain plasticity is limited after the age of twelve years. Thus remedial education may not benefit the secondary school-going child. The management of learning disability in the more time-demanding setting of secondary school is based more on providing provisions and accommodations rather than remediation. These provisions (for example, exemption from spelling mistakes, availing extra time for written tests, dropping a language subject, substituting algebra and geometry with lower grade of mathematics) serve to make the curriculum easier for these students so to make their academic performance commensurate their intellectual ability.

A definite and conclusive diagnosis of learning disability should not be made until the child is in the third grade, or about seven-eight years old as some children may be 'normal' but 'late developers'. Such children usually outgrow their learning problems on their own (unlike learning disability which is a life-long disorder). However, children in the age group of five-seven years who show signs of learning disability on educational assessment should be considered as 'at risk for learning disability' and remedial education should be started (Karande, 2009).

In the year 1996 the state government of Maharashtra was the first in India to formally grant children with SpLD the benefit of availing the necessary provisions to enable them to complete education in regular mainstream schools. Initially these provisions were only given for the standard IX and X examinations; but subsequently in the year 2000 they were given from standard I to XII. Following the good example set by the government of Maharashtra, awareness about the needs of these children has grown in India. Since 1999, the National Educational Boards which conduct the Indian Certificate of Secondary Education and the Central Board of Secondary Education examinations have also formally granted children with SpLD the benefit of availing the necessary provisions. Subsequently, the state governments of Karnataka, Tamil Nadu, Kerala, Gujrat and Goa have also granted these provisions.

CHAPTER 8
UNPROVEN CONTROVERSIAL THERAPIES

There are a number of non-standard treatments used for learning disabilities. In this chapter a number of 'alternative medicine' are presented and deliberated on. The term 'alternative medicine' is commonly used to describe practices used independently or in place of conventional medicine. The term 'complementary medicine' is chiefly used to describe practices used in combination with or to complement conventional medical treatments. The National Center for Complementary and Alternative Medicine (NCCAM) defines Complementary and Alternative Medicine (CAM) as *'a group of diverse medical and health care systems, practices, and products that are not currently part of conventional medicine.'*

In the case of a child with learning disability, parents resort to alternative therapies when their child's condition lacks reliable remediation or remediation shows insufficient progress. Many parents perturbed get advice from well-meaning therapists, teachers or relatives who suggest that perhaps the child would benefit from CAM. Whether the child will benefit from CAM or not is debateable.

Alternative Therapy : Some Examples

Aromatherapy

Aromas can lower stress levels, affect mood, and even change perceptions of pain. The simple scents of fruits and flowers may lighten mild depression; inhaling the aromas of jasmine, rose, or sage is said to ease symptoms of depression. Frankincense and sweet marjoram inhaled or used topically, may be helpful in reducing stress, while lavender and German chamomile oils can bring on a relaxed state.

Movement-based therapies

Educational kinesiology, neuro-developmental therapy, primary movement, brain gym, DDAT programme–these theories maintain that learning difficulties can be caused by primitive reflexes remaining active in the body. The consequence of which is that achieving balance, hand-eye co-ordination, motor control and perceptual skills may be delayed or inhibited. This condition is said to be corrected by a programme of exercises designed to inhibit primary reflexes and thus develop and improve balance, co-ordination

Dietary factors

For the reason that depressive symptoms can be aggravated by nutritional deficiencies, good nutrition is important. The effect of diet on the function and levels of the neurotransmitters those are important for learning and behavior can prove to be very importent. Essential fatty acids (Omega 3 and Omega 6 oils) are said to facilitate maintaining eye and brain function. These essential fatty acids are found in oily fish (e.g. salmon, tuna, and mackerel) and in vegetable oils and seeds (e.g. sunflower, flax, pumpkin and sesame). It has been found that all nutrients influenced delayed paragraph recall but only fat improved attention and only protein improved rate of forgetting (Kaplan, Greenwood, Winocur, and Wolever, 2001). In this way, diet can affect learning and behavior. Malnourished children in India were found to have delays in vision, fine motor skills, language skills and personal-social skills (Vazir, Naidu, and Vidyasagar, 1998). Even in healthy individuals, feelings of fatigue and distress decline thirty minutes after eating a meal regardless of whether the meal was primarily carbohydrate or protein.

Color therapy

Warm colors of yellow, orange, and red stimulate mood in color baths, lighting, room decor and clothing. People with hypertension should avoid too much red. These same colors in food provide anti-oxidants that reduce the effects of mood swings brought on by allergies.

Color light therapy

Color light therapy is being used for children with special needs in Special Needs Centres. Light therapy is being used for children who have learning disabilities. A special colored filter chosen by the individual child when placed over their reading material helps a child learn more. Yellow is the most popular color. Practitioners have revealed that using a blue light at bedtime helps to calm children to sleep and relax and has been used to calm children with Attention Deficit Disorder.

Vision therapy

It is also referred to as visual training or vision training. It is a method attempting to correct or improve presumed ocular disorders, visual processing, and perceptual disorders. One of the forms of vision therapy is referred to as behavioral vision therapy. It is an eye movement and hand-eye coordination training techniques are used to improve visual processing skills, learning efficiency, and visual-motor integration. Behavioral vision therapy is based on the premise that differences in children's visual perceptual motor abilities exist and that these perceptual motor abilities influence cognitive and adaptive skills such as reading, writing, and motor activities used in activities of daily living. Behavioral vision therapy has been recommended to improve visual skills and processing in the belief that this will improve learning disabilities, including speech and language disorders, and nonverbal learning disorders.

Music therapy

Way back in 1976, in USA, a program called 'Music for Children with Reading Learning Disabilities' was created to teach skills necessary in language reading through music, and to evaluate whether the development of music skills resulted in an improvement in language reading skills. The focus in music therapy is on rhythm (developing rhythm patterns through large and small muscle groups), singing (perceiving and comprehending melodic patterns and producing them accurately) and notation (reading and notating). Music has been drawn on with some success to improve math scores for students with learning disabilities. Music has been played to block out background noise while students did math problems (Vernetti and Jacobs, 1972) and music relaxation and visual imagery have been used prior to working on math (Schuster and Vincent, 1980). In view of the fact that each child with a learning disability has different needs, it is necessary for the music teacher to work in partnership with the special educator (Atterbury, 1989). On the basis of the information gathered through this collaboration, the music teacher can then implement appropriate strategies. A few words of caution. A child with sequencing disability may not be able to play a repeated rhythmic pattern on an instrument. A student with a memory disability may not be able to remember a series of numbers for a short time or echo sing a short melody after a model.

Yoga

Practitioners of yoga claim that yoga offers an effective therapeutic choice for children with learning disabilities. Yogic breathing exercises (pranayama) is said to stimulate the central nervous system and strengthen the immune system. In combination with yoga poses (asanas) and deep relaxation, pranayama, facilitates the development of body awareness, balance, memory and concentration. Practitioners claim that students with dyslexia often receive special benefit from practising the yogic eye exercises. They claim that Yogic eye exercises strengthen the optic nerve, relaxes facial muscles and stimulates various centres of the brain. These exercises improves the ability of the eyes to focus and enhance word recognition skills. Eye exercises are only one example of how yoga can be adapted to minimize specific learning deficits; however, Yoga for the Special Child is primarily a holistic therapy, and as such, its main objective is to enhance all areas of a child's development. Five basic areas of practice are given (1) asanas or body postures (2) pranayama or breathing exercises (3) cleansing practices (4) music and sound therapy (5) deep relaxation.

Urudhva Mukha Paschimottanasana Technique

Lie flat on the floor or on a carpet and place your hands straight over the head. Stretch the legs straight, tighten the knees and take a few deep breaths. Exhale and slowly raise the legs together and bring them over the head. Interlock the fingers, clasp the soles and stretch the legs straight up with the knees kept tight. Rest the entire back and the floor. Take three deep breaths. Exhale; lower the legs towards the floor beyond the head by widening the elbows. Try and keep the pelvis as near the floor as possible. Keep the legs tightened at the knees throughout. Rest the chin on the knees. Stay in the position from 30 to 60 seconds, breathing evenly. Exhale and move the legs to the original position. Inhale, release the hands, bring the legs straight to the floor and relax.

Effect

The pose helps improving balance and poise. It also strengthens the back. It brings about steadiness of movements at the musculoskeletal level and helps to calm down and stabilize the mind (Nagarathna, Undated)

Complementary and Alternative Medicine

Most importantly it is vital to remember that learning disability is not a disease and therefore cannot be 'cured' no matter what any doctor or therapist asserts. Moreover, there are no simple solution to alleviate learning disability because of its the complex multifactorial nature as each learning disability encompasses a various problems including reading memory, motor movement and even problems like self-esteem, concentration and so on. There are no simple solutions to alleviate learning disability because of its complex multifactorial nature. Remedial education is a slow and extremely time consuming pursuit and moreover provides no guarantees; parents of children with learning disabilities often turn to alternative treatments.

The term Complementary and Alternative Medicine refers to any therapy that is not provided by orthodox health professionals like doctors, nurses and dentists (NCCAM, 2009). Complementary and Alternative Medicine (CAM) has grown rapidly over the last two decades. However, little is known about the level of CAM use or the type of CAM used by dyslexic children (Bull, 2009).

Alternative medicine is understood to connote treatments that are presented as an option to conventional or Western medical treatments. For example, when cancer patients choose not to have chemotherapy and in its place follow special dietary regime or have ayurvedic and herbal medicines.

Complementary medicine or therapy describes treatments that can be used alongside conventional treatment, for example, osteopathy and Reiki healing, chiropractic and massage therapy.

CAM can be divided into three groups:

1. Acupuncture, chiropractic, osteopathy, herbal medicine and homeopathy all of which had the best professional organisations and training standards. They are regulated professions which means it is illegal for anyone to practice them without being registered with a professional body.

2. Includes therapies that are harmless enough to complement conventional medicine even though supporting evidence was lacking; among these are aromatherapy, Bach flower remedies, massage therapy, meditation, reflexology, shiatsu, healing, nutritional medicine and yoga

3. This group consists of those therapies that are considered scientifically unproven and unregulated. These include ayurveda, traditional Chinese medicine, naturopathy, crystal therapy, iridology, and kinesiology.

The National Center for Complementary and Alternative Medicine's, USA (NCCAM's) grouping of CAM into three sections is as follows (NCCAM, 2007a).

1. Mind and Body
2. Biologically Based Practices

3.   Manipulative and Body-Based Practices

Mind-body medicine centers on the connections with the brain, mind, body, and behavior. It advocates the powerful ways in which emotional, mental, social, spiritual, and behavioral factors can directly affect health. Knowledge of mind-body therapy typically focuses on intervention strategies that are thought to promote health, such as relaxation, hypnosis, visual imagery, meditation. Examples of it are Music therapy, Reiki and Yoga.

Biologically based practices include botanicals, animal-derived extracts, vitamins, minerals, fatty acids, amino acids, proteins, prebiotics and probiotics, live bacteria found in foods such as yoghurt or in dietary supplements, whole diets, and functional foods. Dietary supplements and medicinal herbs have been used by mankind to cure and heal since the beginning of time. In India thousands of botanical plants or parts of a plant are used for their flavour, scent, or potential therapeutic properties. Flowers, leaves, bark, fruit, seeds, stems, and roots had been used for their medicinal effects. Many of these, including digitalis and quinine, form the basis of modern drugs (Goldman. 2001). Examples are ayurvedic medicines, dietary supplements, and flower remedy.

Manipulative and body-based practices focus primarily on the structures and systems of the body, including the bones and joints, the soft tissues, and the circulatory and lymphatic systems. Some of these practices were derived from traditional systems of medicine, such as those from China and India. However some were developed as late as 150 years ago like chiropractic and osteopathic manipulation. Although many practitioners have formal training in the anatomy and physiology of humans, there is significant inconsistency in the training and the approaches of these providers both across and within modalities (NCCAM,

2007). Some example are Reflexology, Massage, Chiropractic and Osteopathic manipulation.

Most therapies are relatively safe, with the exception of acupuncture, chiropractic and herbal medicine which could cause harm in the wrong hands. The author of this book is in agreement with the implementation of new and improved methods of teaching but she believes she owes it to her readers to be cautious when new and alternative methods are recommended. Therefore, the author does not endorse any methods of working with learning disabled children other than teaching which is specific and systematically planned to accommodate the learner's assessed needs. If other non-teaching therapies are being considered, then user should assure themselves as to the scientific validity of these therapies.

Are Complementary and Alternative Medicine Effective?

Before availing of any complementary medical technique, one should be aware that many of these techniques have not been evaluated in scientific studies (Chivers, 2006). Frequently, only incomplete and partial information is presented about their safety and effectiveness. It is always best to speak with your paediatrician or any other medical health professional before starting any new therapeutic technique.

Some contentions that make it hard to prove that an alternative therapy really works include:

i.   the fact that children often improve anyway because of growth and development
ii. the fact that development for particular children may be delayed or may level off for periods of time, resulting in progress occurring slower than usual
iii. the type and severity of each child's disability may vary

iv. the expectations, motivation and experience of each child may
     vary
v.   the expectations, motivation and experience of parents may
     vary
vi. the skills and experience of treating therapists may vary

All of these things may be causing the changes that are
observed, rather than the therapy approach being used. This is
why using an objective scientific method for measuring all of
these things becomes important.

What are the Concerns about Complementary and Alternative Medicine?

The first anxiety about these therapies that comes to a common
person's mind is the way they are marketed. Usually they are
advertised using grandiloquent and high flowing phrases like
'scientific breakthrough' or 'miraculous' progress or 'special
clinic'. Sometimes they make claims that the scientific and the
medical world are involved in a conspiracy to stop the common
man from finding out about their benefits. Most often than not,
they are very expensive and time-consuming treatments. And then
when the parents of the child cannot take it any more they are
blamed for lack of patience and commitment.

Medical professionals are usually apprehensive of such
treatments as they are not well researched (Chivers, 2006). They
report unpublished case histories and testimonials and circumvent
scientific examination of their effectiveness. Frequently, such
treatments are claimed to be 'natural' and have no known side
effects, but this is not always true.

However, Complementary and Alternative Medicine and
therapies send a strong message of hope to the already tired parent
of the learning disabled child. The parents are usually willing to

try any method that insinuates 'something can be done'. They make the caretaker feel optimistic in the face of adversity.

Conclusion

Few high-quality studies have investigated how CAM therapies may affect young people (NCCAM, 2009a). One should be cautioned that results from studies on adults are not applicable to children. It is vital to remember that children are not miniature adults. Their immune and central nervous systems are not fully developed, which can make them respond to treatments differently from adults. Herbs and other dietary supplements may interact with medicines or other supplements. In addition, 'natural' does not necessarily mean 'safe' as CAM therapies can have side effects.

Parents should seek information from scientific studies about how safe and effective a specific CAM therapy is in children. However, since few, if any, rigorous studies on young people exist, additional scientific studies are needed. Anecdotes and testimonials (personal stories) about CAM therapies are common and can be compelling, but they are not evidence.

Parents of a child with learning disabilities may consult the pediatrician about the utility of unconventional therapies such as optometric training, eye muscle exercises, tinted colored lenses, anti-motion sickness medication for vestibular dysfunction, sensory integration therapy, chiropractic manipulation, mega-vitamin therapy, or sucrose-restricted diet; and of complementary medicine (homeopathy, ayurvedic) to treat their child's disability. None of these have proved to be effective when subjected to double-blind controlled clinical trials (Karande et al, 2007). The paediatrician can help parents become better-informed consumers.

CHAPTER 9

WHAT PARENTS CAN DO

Most experts are of the opinion that parents of children with learning disability usually do not have an adequate amount of knowledge about learning disability and its management. This opinion is formed over the years of interactions with parents, who accompany their children to our clinic for diagnosis and during follow up (Karande et al, 2007). He maintains that he and his colleagues have come across parents who:

1. Did not believe the diagnosis of learning disability and mostly did not accept it
2. Had not started remedial education but instead employed a regular teacher to give private tuitions. The tuition teacher had training in remedial education
3. Discontinued remedial education within a few weeks or months for lack of perceived benefit
4. Refused to take advantage of provisions granted by the Educational boards. This is done with the view that availing this option would restrict future career options of their progeny. For example, at present in our educational system, a child who has opted for lower grade of mathematics cannot later opt for a career in engineering.

On the other hand for years the family member is considered by many educators as troublesome. A parent is the child's first teacher. The parent or/and the extended family member is always there to give encouragement, words of praise or correction. I believe nobody holds more vested interest in the child's welfare as does the family member.

Having a child with a learning disability is even more challenging than raising a child without one, and certainly more frustrating. Karande and associates (2007) suggest that a sympathetic and supportive home environment is one of the factors that can positively determine the outcome of learning disability in a school-going child. Moreover, parents are a child's first and best teachers.

Some Positive Steps for Parents

1. Learning disabilities take many forms. Learn as much as you can about the different types of learning disability. As a knowledgeable, informed parent, you will be better able to communicate with teachers about your child, help your child with schoolwork, and develop strategies to help him/ her come through social situations effectively and survive.
2. Keep in contact with your child's teacher. Let them be aware of your child's behavior at home. It is helpful for the teacher to know the child's favorite subjects or lessons or know about a class he/she has particularly enjoyed. Parents also play an essential role in working with teachers to develop directive and behavioral policies that can be used both in school and at home. Talk to specialists in your school (e.g., special education teacher) about methods for teaching your child.
3. Repetition is the key for all your child's learning. Repeat! Repeat! Repeat!

4. Keep a 'positive feature profile' or a 'forte account' of what your child does well.
   Find out and emphasize what the child's strengths and interests are. Give the child positive feedback and lots of opportunities for practice. This can be important for your child at school and on a personal level. More often than not we tend to focus on the areas in which a child needs to improve and thus invariably forget what the child is good at. A 'forte account' can help teachers and parents remember areas in which the child excels and that can be used to build curriculum that is meaningful to the child. A 'forte account' or a 'positive feature profile' is useful when parents would like to get over the times when a child is failing or cannot cope and is feeling frustrated.

5. Even when a child accepts that he or she has a learning disability, the child may not realize how it will affect his or her life. Parents should help their child understand that the learning disability may mean he or she will have difficulty reading, that others may become frustrated with the child, or that the child may misread social cues, which can impact his or her social life.

6. Involve your child in extra-curricular activities. Some children with learning disabilities have a difficult time making friends as they usually have one or many of these common behavioral characteristics of individuals with learning disabilities:

   i. Inability to interpret environment and social cues
   ii. Poor judgment, little thought about logical consequences
   iii. Poor impulse control
   iv. Need for immediate gratification
   v. Inability to set realistic priorities and goals
   vi. Inappropriate conclusions due to deficient reasoning ability
   vii. Illogical reasons for actions

vii. Inability to develop meaningful relationships with others

viii. Immature and 'bossy' behavior

ix. Low frustration tolerance resulting in disruptive behavior

Moreover their day is usually planned with remedial classes, thus leaving not enough time and energy for making friends. By getting your child involved in extra-curricular activities offers an opportunity in which your child can achieve success, as well as gain new friends. Besides his/her school learning, find what your child is especially good at. Nurture this talent, whether it is in the area of sports, art, music or dancing. This will help raise self-esteem. The child's success in this other field may also raise your child's respect in the minds of her/his friends which also plays an important part in a child's self-worth.

7. Keep your expectations for your child high but at the same time be pragmatic. It is particularly important that you let your child know that you believe in him/her. Only then will you be able to teach your child to believe in him/herself. Praise your child for both the small steps and big leaps in the right direction

8. Children with learning disabilities are often very creative and insightful. By asking their opinions and allowing them to figure out the answers to problems, you let them know you trust their intellect and their judgment.

9. Teach your child self-advocacy skills. They should learn to ask for the help when they 'need' it. Like asking to sit in the most advantageous seat in the classroom that is, if the teacher talks with her back to the child the child may not understand the lesson properly.

10. Teach your child organizational skills, study skills, and learning strategies. These help all students but are particularly helpful to those with learning disability. Find a specific place

for your child to do homework that has lots of light, silence, and plenty of work space. Establish a regular time with your child to do homework-developing a schedule helps avoid procrastination. Practice school-taught skills at home. Relate homework to your child's everyday life. Like having the child repeat the directions given by you or reading to the child helps with receptive language and then asking what, when, and where questions from the story. For example, having the child repeat directions back to you.

11. Join or form a group of parents with similar children who face if not similar problems, at least comparable problems. You can gain useful information from other parents too. In addition to that, they can be a source of support in times of stress. You can share research, practical advice, your experiences and moral support.

12. Consider counseling if your child seems overly sad, frustrated or angry, and is having difficulty dealing with these feelings.

13. Remember to praise your child's achievements. Knowing that he/she's doing something correctly, will give your child the confidence to try new things. Stress on persistence, praise when praise is due and your child will find his/her own way to flourish and succeed.

CHAPTER 10

WHAT THE CLASS TEACHER CAN DO

The teacher makes a huge difference in the lives of a student. This is especially true for the student who learns differently from his /her peers. Students with learning disabilities often require individual attention especially in terms of accommodations and modifications.

More often than not, a learning disability is distinctive to the individual and can be manifested in a variety of ways. Consequently, accommodations for a specific student must be personalized to the individual. Similarly, students with learning disabilities are often as smart as their peers, but since they process information differently, they need additional support to compensate for their disability. Teachers who are aware of learning differences in their students can help these students learn better in the classroom. They can help by:

1. By knowing all there is to know about learning disabilities
2. Being perceptive and sympathetic to the fact that learning styles differ for every student
3. Setting up a learning environment that supports different learning styles

4. Knowing the correct time to intervene when learning becomes difficult

Below are some suggestions of classroom adjustment, assignment reconsideration, and examination accommodations that may be recommended for students with a learning disability.

1. Teach study skills specific to the subject area – organizing (for example, assignment schedule), textbook reading and note taking (finding main idea / detail, mapping, outlining)
2. Teach specific methods of self-monitoring (for example, stop-look-listen to check careless errors in spelling, arithmetic, and reading.) Have the student proof-read finished work before submission.
3. Allow the student to have additional time to complete in-class assignments, particularly writing assignments.
4. Help student to get organized. Teach them 'place for everything and everything in its place'. Frequently examine notebooks. Provide positive reinforcement for good organization.

If the child has:

1. Difficulty following a plan, has unrealistic high aspirations and lacks follow-through; sets out to 'get full marks, ends up failing in other words sets unrealistic goals

    Then a teacher can:

    i. Help the child in planning enduring goals and further breaking the goal into practical and realistic parts.
    ii. Have the student set unambiguous timeliness of what he/she needs to do to achieve these goals.

2. Difficulty in sequencing and completing steps to accomplish specific tasks like writing a test paper, organized paragraphs, division problem, composition and so on; moves from one uncompleted task to another without completing either of

them; difficulty prioritizing from most to least important Difficulty completing assignments:

i. Reduce the assignment into manageable sections
ii. Break up task into workable and obtainable steps and provide examples
iii. List all steps necessary to complete each assignment
iv. Arrange for the student to have a 'study buddy'

3. Difficulty following instructions:

i. First, be sure you have the student's attention before giving directions.
ii. Use oral directions with written directions.
iii. Give one direction at a time.
iv. Quietly repeat the directions to the student after they have been given to the rest of the class.
v. Check for understanding by having the student repeat the directions.

4. Difficulty sustaining effort and accuracy over time:

i. Reduce assignment length and strive for quality rather than quantity.
ii. Give the student a time limit for a small unit of work with positive reinforcement for accurate completion.
iii. Use a contract and timer for self-monitoring.

5. Difficulty with any task that requires memory:

i. Unite reading, verbalizing, writing and doing.
ii. Teach memory techniques as a study strategy like mnemonics, visualization, oral rehearsal, several repetitions and over-learning.

6. Confusion with non-verbal cues like misreading body language and facial expressions:

i. Directly teach non-verbal cues, model and

ii.   have student practice reading cues in a safe setting

7. Confusion with written material, involves difficulty finding the main idea from a paragraph or attaching too much importance to negligible details:

i.   Provide student with a copy of reading material with main ideas underlined or highlighted
ii. Provide an outline of important points from reading material
iii. Teach main-idea and details of concepts
iv. Teach and emphasize key words
v.   Encourage use of tape recorder

8. Difficulty sustaining attention to tasks and is easily distracted by extraneous stimuli:

i.   Break up activities into small units
ii. Reduce distractions
iii. Reward attention

9. Messy or sloppy work:

i.   Teach organizational skills
ii. Provide examples for what you want the student to do
iii. Establish a daily routine
iv. Make job sheets for the student which has list of daily, weekly and monthly assignments.
v.   Give reward points for tidy and orderly notebook
vi. Arrange for a peer or a 'study buddy' who will help him/her with organization.

10. Poor handwriting; often mixing cursive with manuscript and capitals with low-case letters. Difficulty with fluency in handwriting. May have good letter/word production but very slow and laborious:

    i. Do not reprimand a student for mixing cursive and manuscript.

    ii. Accept any method of production

    iii. Allow shorter assignments, encourage quality not quantity

    iv. Permit for a scribe; mark them for content, not handwriting

    v. Allow the use of computer

    vi. Consider alternative methods for student assignments like tape recorder or oral reports

    vii. Use pencil with rubber grip

11. Clearly noticeable inattentive behavior in classroom like underachievement, daydreaming, 'not being there'; difficulty participating in class without being interruptive and working quietly; inappropriate seeking of attention like the student clowns around, displays attention-seeking behavior, interrupts; frequent excessive talking

    i. Seat student in close proximity to the teacher.

    ii. Reward appropriate behavior like when the student is being good and is displaying appropriate behavior and reinforce.

    iii. Be sure to have the student's attention before giving directions.

    iv. Ask student to repeat the directions

    v. Teach the student hand signals and make use of them to convey to the student when to talk and when not to talk.

12. Difficulty remaining seated and frequently fidgets with hands, feet or objects

    i. Give the student frequent opportunities to get up and move around.

    ii. Have space for movement

    iii. Allow alternative movement when possible

13. Anxiety under pressure and competition be it athletic or academic

    i. Emphasis on the joy of the endeavor, enjoyment of learning for ones self
    ii. Learning rather than competition with others

14 Inappropriate behaviors in a team or large group sport or athletic activity, often has difficulty when turn in games and/or group situations occur.

    i. Give the student a responsible job like being the team captain.
    ii. Allow him/her to care of and distribute the balls.
    iii. Be the score keeper.
    iv. Keep the student near the teacher.

15. Recurrent involvement in physically dangerous activities without considering possible consequences:

    i. Stress on Stop-Look-Listen
    ii. And 'red says stop, yellows says get set and green says go.'
    iii. Pair with responsible peers

16. Low self-esteem, negative comments about self and others, lack of confidence to attempt tasks or complete them:

    i. Allow opportunities for the student to show his strength
    ii. Train student for self-monitoring
    iii. Reinforce improvements
    iv. Give positive recognition

17. Difficulty during exams or test:

    i. Teach test-taking skills and strategies
    ii. Use test format that the student is most comfortable with.

iii. Make available the alternative of an oral exam
iv. Permit extra time for testing; typically time and one half to double time
v. Let the child complete the exams in a room or in the area of the room with reduced distractions
vi. Urge the school to authorize the assistance of a reader and/or a scribe for exams
vii. Permit the use of a calculator for exams and to use rough paper during exams

CHAPTER 11

FLASHBACK AND FLASHFORWARD

The following are two real life stories of my students, both of whom I taught as a special educational needs co-ordinator, for a period of twenty-two months, during my doctoral research. The aim of my class was to enhance life skills in children with specific learning difficulties (SpLD), in a school in Mumbai. On the principles of life skills enhancement. I built the lessons of the class to augment inner capacities in order to meet the challenges of education. The core set of skills (WHO 1997: p.1) I aimed to enhance were:

- Communication
- Coping with emotion
- Coping with stress
- Creative thinking
- Critical thinking
- Decision-making
- Empathy

- Interpersonal skills
- Problem solving

Children undergo great stress when they have to be tested for SpLD. This is especially true for Indian students. So, as to avert a stressful situation for the children I had decided to accept the school's resource room records of SpLD. The significant others, who played a vital role in my study were the children's parents, class teachers and the special educational needs co-ordinator (SENCO) who assisted me to draw their portraits. This collaboration was indispensable as I strongly believe that a child's education, whether intellectual, emotional or moral, is a group effort of all those who interact one way or another with the child.

The zeal I have for teaching and to accomplish something for the 'child in need' shaped my work. I believe that if:

'...teachers can begin to think of themselves as among those able to kindle the light or among those willing to confront the dread and keep alive the sense of "a possible happiness", they might find themselves revisioning their life projects, existing proactively in the world...'

(Greene, 2003a: internet
source without page no.)

SARLA

Imagine a happy, bubbly girl with a huge smile on her face. Think of a jumping puppy dancing around you, moving in rings around you or going away for a short time but the minute someone comes near you, she always comes back to take her place. She is someone who happily holds your hands, and you will feel the warmth coming through. Her hair was always partly tied back, the front part was and the rest left loose. As if she was finding a middle path, a compromise, between a school rule that asks girls to tie their hair and the fashion statement which suggests that smart girls leave their hair loose.

Self Portrait (done in the last drama class)

- She is dyslexic, with short-memory problem
- Cannot complete a sentence without help; regularly speaks in incomplete sentences; 'I always do only' she said when I asked her if she would try to remember something
- Has a mild speech problem (cannot say 'sh' and 'rr')
- Does not perform well in scholastic tasks, like the three 'r's
- Has a concentration problem

She attends remedial classes in school.

She often wears 'colored' clothes for my class, even though the school rule states that all children should wear the uniform to my drama class. My drama class took place on Saturday, a school holiday. I asked her mother about that and her mother said that the children should be allowed to wear 'normal' clothes on Saturday, as everyone in the building enquired what class the child attends on holidays. Her mother is very glad that her child comes for these classes; however, she is at the same time embarrassed that the child needs extra help. This embarrassment reflects in the child's attitude too. The reply I got from her as an excuse for not wearing her uniform was: 'Miss, Saturday no one should wear uniform.'

There is a lot of discrepancy in what she actually is and what everyone around reveals about her. She has a tendency to cling and that was the first sign of her lack of confidence I noticed. She is one child who always has to stand near me; there is no way she will give up that place to any one. No amount of persuading could make her change that place. Ultimately after a few classes I gave up, I let her stand near me if that is what made her comfortable!

There are other signs of immaturity and low self confidence too, some that upset, worried and embarrassed her mother. Her mother said in an interview with me that Sarla is very childish and does not behave like children her age do. She lacks the maturity of a normal ten year old. Her friends are younger than her as she cannot communicate with children in her age group. She is not well behaved in public places; she behaves very childishly in restaurants whereas her cousins of the same age behave acceptably.

I noticed that sometimes Sarla does behave childishly, however not always. I believe this kind of behavior was manifested because of her lack of self-confidence. However, in a class of only ten children all within her age group, her behavior seems normal. Her drama class friends treat her just the way they treat the others. It must be observed that in my class there is no competition and this is one of the reasons she enjoys coming. She does not have to put on a mask and hide behind it.

Her lack of confidence was evident from her behavior in the class. For example, when I asked them to do the worksheets, Sarla was the only one to ask for an eraser even before they had started writing. I asked her, 'Sarla, why do you need an eraser?' To which she replied, 'I think'. I said, 'Why do you think? Why do you think beta [child]? Why do you need it even before you start? First you have to write something, only then you can erase. Why do you think of erasing something before you start?' Sarla said laughing nervously, 'Because it can be when you will not give.' To which I said, remembering that they will soon be using fountain pens in school, 'What will you do when you will write with a pen.' Sarla said, 'Cut it, cut it.'

Her parents realize that she has a reading and writing problem. However, they do not know how to handle that. Her mother does realize her confidence needs to be built up. However, her father is always discouraging her. Her father told me that he is very proud of his son; 'man of few words' he calls his son, like himself. Her mother requested me to meet the father alone and convince him not to say anything that could lower Sarla's self esteem. He seemed to be 'putting Sarla down' all the time. The mother did not approve of his behavior but could not do much about it.

Self portrait done in first class

Her mother was perpetually worried about her school marks. Her mother told me 'One thing I realised just two days back. It [her confidence] was not there. I now realise that..... I was...shocked when I got her exam paper...and she didn't ever...which was ten simple sentences or fifteen simple sentences, several questions were directs, each and every answer is different but because of her inconfidence (sic) [lack of confidence] or whatever you feel, she didn't have confidence in reading.. so she didn't attempt them, the question... as the teacher didn't read it out to her. In English she ... she attempted the comprehension and Hindi she didn't even try.'

The SENCO's opinion was that Sarla was shy and quiet in a group though not in a one-to-one interaction. She had difficulty in mixing with children, and preferred to be alone. She does not interact well in a group situation. She was therefore very comfortable in the drama class, which had only ten students. When I had asked them during reflection time why they were comfortable in my class she said, 'Because there are less students.' She probably has an unhappy relationship with her class friends during school hours and their behavior (maybe teasing or bullying) towards her because of her school marks and /or her childish behavior.

She compensates for her lack of self-esteem sometimes by speaking just for the sake of speaking, as if she has to respond even if she does not know the answer. Once she said suddenly, 'Little different, we have to do'. I asked 'why' not because I was surprised she spoke, but because she sometimes speaks without really understanding, merely for the sake of speaking. To which she replied, 'This is not good little. No, catch, catch why will we tell where we like?'

Her language development was weak and tends to speak in short sentences, which sometimes do not mean much. Grammatically her sentences are incorrect but one must understand that even though she studies in an English medium school her mother tongue is Gujarati. Once in 'Continuing the Story..' session she wanted to say the nursery rhyme, Twinkle Twinkle little star! Once she said, 'No, catch, catch why will we tell where we like?'

This was little Sarla at ten years. I taught her for over two years. She attended my 'learning life skills through drama' class. The program was very effective and there were vast changes in the girl. From the inconfident girl with low self–esteem, she blossomed into very confident girl. She became excellent at story-telling and would sincerely and wholly participate in the class. Her creative thinking and skills of empathy were augmented as was her understanding of 'self'.

With the enhancement in her life-skills, her behavior changed and she showed signs of developing maturity. Her confidence improved and she started making friends with the children her age in the building she lived in. She could even understand the concept of social ostracism in school and it did not bother her as much as it did when we first started the class.

A new friend and a nice teacher

In October, nearly twenty-one months after we started the drama module, I handed the power position of the class over to the children. The children and I negotiated that each child would conduct a class of his/her choice. Sarla chose the mask making and the 'understanding of the self' lessons for her class. She took the students back to the mask making class and each of the children made their own mask after discussing and reflecting on the class in which they chose their personal metaphors. The following story is in Sarla's voice as she conducted the class. The story is based on the analysis of transcript and data in class. 'I remember the old days...' is a critique of the Sarla's development from the days when she followed me around as described earlier, to the time when she confidently performed in the dance-drama, directed the same, and conducted a successful class. The 'wise-one' in the story is me and the rest are her classmates.

In Which Sarla becomes the Magician

I hope you like listening to stories... this is a story of a newly initiated magician. I am the young magician and my name is Sarla. I have an assistant, the Wise-one. I was going to perform magic for the first time and help all the others to find themselves.

No... the Wise-one had already began the chanting of the spell a long time back. What I was going to do is see if we could find ourselves without the help of the Wise-one.

I had decided to do 'The Magic of the Masks'. My assistant, the Wise-one had got all the materials ...paper plates, paints, brushes, gum and scissors....

We all knew 'The Magic of the Masks'; we had done it before when we became cats. But I remember that time we were not colorful. We were pale reproductions of ourselves. We looked nearly like each other.

What an important job I had today! Nearly twenty-one months since we started our journey. I was scared ...nervous, supposing no one listened to me. The Wise-one could control the wind-Samir, bring Nihar-the fog out into the sun, and help Lali-the little one to grow. And me, Sarla – the simple one, I was not plain any more. I am sure you can understand that performing magic in front of the other ten travellers was a task I could not have even imagined I would be able to do in the beginning of our journey.

I remember the old days when I followed the Wise-one everywhere she went, I was like her puppy dog. I did not allow anyone to hold her hand or sit next to her. In the magic circle, when we had our meetings, I had to sit next to her. Now, I was slowly taking tiny steps and moving away on my own, like a young bird ready to fly out of the safety of the nest.

'The Magic of the Masks' helps convey us to another world, stirring up our powers of imagination in the search of self-knowledge. At this point I must make it clear; masks could be used as a disguise to hide ones self. But I have used 'The Magic of the Masks' to help my fellow travellers find themselves again.

The Wise-one suggested we all try geometrical designs and colors we liked. The Wise-one is growing old and forgetful ...she forgot we had already decided our secret identity. We were Mr. Rabbit, I am Raat Rani(my identity), wild animals like Running Leopard and Chatterbox Monkey.

Mr. Rabbit

Queen of Hearts

Nihar insisted he was the national flower of India, the lotus, because he did not want to become a Lion again ...' Shenal transformed into a sunflower ...Mukul became a rabbit ...Samir and Kanha ...became wild and exotic animals and I metamorphosed into a queen of hearts...

The magic worked! This time we had become brightly colored and had very definite identities. We were not like the pale sun on a cloudy monsoon day. We were like the vibrant sun in the Indian summer.

Sarla often calls me to tell me of her progress. And invariably her mother comes on line to talk too. Her parents are really proud of the way she has developed. Her learning disability is still there with her. However, she has learned to over come her problems. Sarla now has completed her 10 and 12 standard board examinations with 70 percent and 65 percent respectively. She is a very pretty adult who loves to dress up and since she was good at drawing she has taken up Fashion designing. I am really proud of my student and am glad she has kept in touch with me through all these years (nearly for 9 years). She always remembers to wish me on festive days especially Teachers' Day.

NIHAR

Nihar is like someone standing in a thick fog. I can see him but yet I cannot! He is relaxed in class but does not participate in solo activities. At the same time when he is working with his friend Samir, he performs. They create stirring plays together.

An extremely quiet boy; a big boy, bigger (physically) than the rest of them. He therefore, gives the impression of an older child. He gives the impression of a child you can depend on to do things, like run errands getting things, but definitely not take responsibility in and of the class. He is very good at drawing. Importantly he enjoys drawing. His drawings are the most mature developmentally as compared to the rest of the class.

Portrait of Samir done by Nihar at ten years of age

His mother and sister came to meet me for the parent's interview. His sister accompanied his mother because his mother does not know how to write and was unsure of herself. His sister is presently studying in junior college. Both agreed that the child had friends in the building and mostly of the same age group. However, the mother said that Nihar is a loving child who likes to play with children younger than him. She says, 'Bahut pyaar kaarta hai' [is warm and loving] with children younger than him. Teacher 'ke pyaar ka bhooka hai' [desires to be loved by his teachers].

In the parent's interview, his mother said his favorite past time was playing with toy cars, likes playing with his cars, and doesn't like to study. He knows the intricate details about cars. Even before we know about the latest car he knows, and can point it out on the road. Every object is like a car to him; even his pencil sharpener. When he is sleepy, he puts his cars in a line and then sleeps. He dreams of buying a bungalow and swanky cars which is expressed in, 'proud se reheneka' [living with pride and dignity]. He is a very proud boy.

All his mother desired was that he gets better marks in school. Her query concerning the drama class was merely focused in that direction. 'Will these classes help him to get good marks? Would that make him cleverer?' she asked me.

He is learning disabled and has additionally ADHD (Attention Deficit Hyperactivity Disorder) as reported by SENCO, but was not on any form of medication. He is Dyslexic and has problem with written work and is weak at spellings. But he did not have behavior problem. Low concentration. In school, he does not move from his place in class, however after 6 months of one-to-one interaction, he has started to approach the teacher if he had some problems. He needs to be highly motivated to do any work. The SENCO told me that he usually said 'no' to start a new task, and needs lots of encouragement and re-enforcement to be persuaded to start. The SENCO's report suggested that he is soft spoken, is weak in speech, his pronunciation is weak and maybe as a result of that he does not speak much. She also suggests that he is also weak at phonetics. However, his class teachers' do not perceive any speech problem. One of his teachers added to the query concerning verbal communication behavior saying, 'Hardly opens his mouth, no response'.

His lack of confidence could be perceived from the beginning of my classes. Even when we played a simple game of 'Tell your name and strike a pose' he took the option of 'I pass'. He chose not to speak. His sentences are always punctuated by aaah. He is extremely quiet. This was confirmed by the class teacher who said that he is quiet, not talkative in class. He mumbles while talking and that his speech was jumbled. His parents suggested that he stammers. Nihar told me during our initial sessions, 'I don't like to talk.' In the drama class Nihar was very quiet. During circle time/reflection time he rarely said more than a sentence especially when we sat in a circle. Nihar's such behavior made me relax the rule of sitting in a circle during circle/reflection time. I noticed that when we did not sit in a circle Nihar usually sat in the back with his friend Samir. And then from the back, hidden behind other children, Nihar would express himself. Once during reflection time he confided in me, 'Miss, I like to draw.' I discovered later on that Nihar could draw very well and was especially talented at drawing. This was something neither did his teachers, SENCO nor his parents had known or reported to me.

All the significant others like his teachers, SENCO and his parents did not report that he had low concentration. This was a problem, which did not surface in the drama class. I believe this was due to the inherent nature of the class, which did not have a lecture format and was a multisensory mode of learning. Drama did not require my students to sit in one place and was action oriented. However, Nihar did not always 'perform' but I noticed that he was always observing the activities in class and was paying full attention to his friends' actions and me.

He presented no overt signs of behavior problem like truancy, loneliness, isolation or violent behavior in my class. However, his teacher suggested that he fidgets all the time, chews on his pencils and was extremely restless. She replied that he bullies and tries to dominate other children during group activities. She told me, 'Earlier about two years ago, Nihar was very aggressive, would beat other children, but this year he is quiet in class, there are few complaints from other children about him.' Another teacher told me that he bites his nails and is constantly restless. She also suggested that he bullies and tries to dominate other children during group activities. At home he would often take out his anger on his toys and his mother claimed that he was jealous of others' toys.

Now, approximately 22 months after I started my −'learning life skills through drama class', the children have all become more comfortable. Nihar is regular in his attendance. Is it not peculiar? The more comfortable they (the children especially the shy ones) are, the more regular they become and the more regular they are the more comfortable they become....

The most regular children in my class progressed at a steady pace. In the beginning it was difficult to make Nihar do anything or say anything. He, however, was always paying attention. I did not pressurise him, rather gave him an opportunity to take part and leaving the option of 'I pass'.

Nihar has really gained from being regular. He started off by just being there. I kept thinking that at least he is watching the others. One can learn just by listening. I remember telling his mother and sister that they should not worry if he does not actively participate in the beginning. For a shy child, sometimes it is enough that he/she attends the class and watches the others and listens. For a shy child, sometimes it is enough that he/she attends the class and watches the others and listens. I noticed that (and assessed from the peer assessment scores in my class) all the children in my drama class thought that Nihar worked well with the group. Like Sarla he to could understand the concept of social ostracism in school and it did not bother him as much now. This is because his self-esteem was augmented with his improved 'understanding of Self'. A greater understanding of emotions and enhanced skills of empathy made Nihar a relaxed and calmer child, as if he did not have to fight with the world all the time.

In creative thinking skills, for example, Nihar had progressed in traits like curiosity, internal locus of control, ability to defer judgement, commitment to task and sense of identity as an originator. The last characteristic surfaced when he could demonstrate his skill in drawing. Nihar drew excellent figures in the diary the children maintained, he drew different emotions as they learnt them, instead of just writing them.

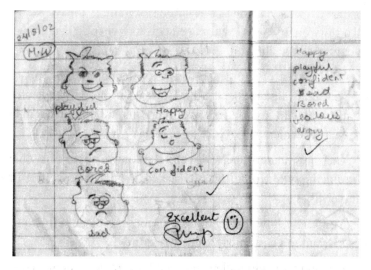

Pages from Nihar's diary – Emotional Understanding lesson

During class I always used an audio-recorder to record the proceedings in class. One day the students all wanted to hear their recorded voices. Nihar was the first one to say he wanted to hear what we have recorded. So I asked him to speak, to say something, which I could record after which we could re-wind the tape and listen. A year back I'm sure he would not have said a thing. Samir would have demonstrated what to do and Nihar would have smiled but definitely not done anything. However, this time he started telling us about a soldier whose first death anniversary was commemorated in their building. I was surprised when Nihar said he wanted to speak and record his voice. Nihar was an extremely quiet boy. His amelioration from a quiet child, who was nearly inactive and stayed in the background, to a child who took the first step in class was like a dream come true for me. The Girl in Nihar's story is me.

Nihar's Story

It is more than a year since we started storytelling, today I want to tell a story on my own. I don't need Girl to give me a beginning or an emotion or a situation.

'Girl, in our building... A man who was not married, his one year became.' I started speaking slowly. But no one understood what I wanted to say so I repeated, 'Girl, in our building ...a man's one-year became.'

Girl now understands us well; she knows some of us have a problem with words. So she asked me if I meant the first anniversary.

You know how I sometimes am not sure of how to express what I want to I just said, 'Arr ... arr ...army ...'

Girl immediately understood that I meant death anniversary.

I wanted so much to share the story with everyone but I was struggling with words. That doesn't bother Girl.

Remember I told you last time, Girl is so curious she always wants to know more.

So she started asking me questions like; He lived in your building? When did he die? How did he die?

Now that is what I call making it easy! I could get my ideas together and continue my story. Sachin, the soldier was up in the mountains at a height of 300 feet. And he slipped, and fell.

'Ohh my God!!' exclaimed Girl.

'You know he was going to become a Major on the fifteenth of August.' I said.

Girl and everybody thought I had finished my story. But no, I had more to tell... and that was the most interesting part of the story.

'And...' I continued trying to get everybody's attention.

'We tell no...? That pundit [astrologer] ...'

'Pundit told that ...'

'He will ...only ...Ahhhhh...'

'Means...'

'Live...'

'Means...'

'He will...'

'We tell no...Bachgaya...' [in Hindi it means 'to be saved']

Girl didn't understand what I was saying and asked, 'He won't become ...?'

'Ahhh ...'

'Taaaa...'

'Paaaa...' I struggled

Snehal thought that was funny. And started imitating me, 'taa... pa...'

Girl corrected her, 'Don't do that.' But I don't mind I know they are my friends and not really, really laughing at me. And now I am also more sure of myself. So I went on...

'Pundit told only three times...he will be saved...this

Ahh ...How we tell ...Means first time... in camp a bomb burst...then second time ...ahh ...tha ...'

Like Sarla, Nihar too has passed his 10th and 12th boards. And is presently studying for his Bachelors in Mass Media degree.

PROVISIONS FOR STUDENTS WITH LEARNING DISABILITIES

Provisions for students with Learning Disabilities studying in school upto 12th standard issued by Maharashtra Government School Education Department.

Maharashtra Government
School Education Department
G.R.No. SSC 1099/(151/99) HSE-2
Mantralaya Extension, Mumbai 400 032.
Dated November 28, 2000

Subject: 1.	Maharashtra State Education, Research and Training Centre, Pune Circular No. 96-97/3334, Dated 30 July 1996
Subject: 1.	Subject and Examination schedule for students with Learning Disabilities and curriculum booklet, November 1996.
Subject: 1.	G.R.No. S.S.C. 1098/5787/(318/98) HSC-to, dated 8 July 1999

G.R.: Among the disabled students studying upto 12th standard, dyslexics, dysgraphics and dyscalculics are included. The Government was considering passing an all-inclusive G.R for all the educational concessions given to educate only compromised students. According to the G.R., educationally compromised school students will get following educational concessions:

1. For students with Learning Disabilities of standard 1st to standard 9th and standard 11th, along with the written test, the students shall also have an oral test for unit and semester examinations.

2. All students with Learning Disabilities of standard 1st to 12th shall be allowed to have 30 minutes (1/2 hour) more than allotted time for all written tests.

3. Students with Learning Disabilities, for standard 10th and 12th examinations, can choose the centre close to their residence.

4. These students are exempted from drawing figures, maps and graphs in written examination and the marks for these questions and sub questions (geometry, science and geography) should appropriately be converted.

5. These students can produce completion certificates for the practical from the recognised institutes for certain subjects such as work experience, social service and technical subjects where practicals are necessary.

6. Only failed learning disabled students, should obtain maximum 20 marks for passing in one or more subjects.

7. Instead of three languages, dyslexic and dysgraphic students can opt for two languages and one subject from the subjects included under work experience.

8. Students with dyscalculia are allowed to give examination of 7th standard mathematics (75 marks) and work experience (75 marks) total 150 marks instead of algebra and geometry.

9. Learning disabled students are exempted from spelling mistakes and mathematical calculation mistakes (writing numbers in wrong order).

Regarding this, Regional Educational Deputy Director should certify the student as learning disabled as per the medical certificate. The concerned educational authorities (primary/secondary) should give proper directions to the concerned school headmasters and see to it that the student is not deprived of approved provisions.

The concerned divisional boards will see to it that at the time of 10th and 12th examinations the concerned authorities will get proper suggestions and confirm that the deserving students get government approved provisions.

http://www.disabilityindia.org/LDConcessions.html

INSTRUCTIONS TO SCHOOLS

Instructions sent to the principals of all schools by the Office of the Deputy Director of Education, to be followed in case of students with Learning Disabilities. Dated May 1997.

Free Translation of Circular NO. DDE/HS-5/154-14

Circular No. DDE/HS-5/15414- Dated 17-5-97

To,

The Principals / Headmistresses
Of all Recognised, Aided / Unaided Schools.

Subject: Meeting held on 16.5.97 regarding Dyslexia, in the presence of Honourable Minister of Transport Shri Pramod Navalkar

All the recognised aided and unaided schools in Greater Bombay Division are hereby informed that there are some Learning Disabled (LD) students studying in their schools. Their learning disability is an invisible handicap which may include dyslexia, dysgraphia and/or dyscalculia.

These children are physically normal like other children and their disability is not externally visible. They are not mentally retarded nor do they have a psychological weakness. Their intelligence is like that of any average child or even better. They have a specific problem due to which the brain is unable to analyse/ interpret correctly the message received by it due to which they make mistakes in writing and numerical calculations. Because of this learning disability, they are neglected and lag behind in their studies.

A meeting was called on 16.5.97 in the presence of Honourable Minister for Transport Shri Pramod Navalkar to discuss ways to assist these LD children to overcome their disability so that they do not lag in their studies or get left out of the mainstream of education. The following instructions have been put forth with respect to the points raised at the said meeting:-

Action should be initiated as per the circular dated 29.12.95 of the Maharashtra State Board of Secondary and Higher Secondary Education and Government order dated 27.03.97

A. **Dyslexia and Dysgraphia**–The students in the category may be permitted to opt for any two languages out of the first, second and third language group. However, out of these two one language should be English (as first or third language) if they are willing to opt for the third language, they can do so, otherwise they have to opt for one subject of Work Experience which will be for 100 marks. The examination of this Work Experience subject will be conducted by the Board.

B. **Dyscalculia**–This category of students will have the option to take instead of Mathematics (150 marks) an Arithmetic paper for std 7 level for 75 marks and a Work Experience subject (not the same as the work experience offered in lieu of language) another 75 marks. Dyscalculia students can be provided with a writer for Arithmetic. The writer has to be a student studying in or equivalent to std. 6. These students will be granted additional 30 minutes time to solve their papers.

C. **Dyslexia and Dysgraphia**–These students will be provided a writer for their written exam and also 30 minutes extra time of solving their question papers.

These students with learning disability should be examined by a Neurologist of a certified centre on the recommendation of a Paediatrician / Special Educator. The Board has a specific medical certificate to be issued by a Neurologist and countersigned by the District Civil Surgeon.

1. Students of Std. IX and X to be given concessions as per A, B and C above.
2. There should be a special sympathetic consideration for such students.
3. If any of the symptoms of Dyslexia, Dysgraphia or Dyscalculia are observed in class, parents must be personally informed. Parents must also be guided to ensure that the child has no psychological problems.
4. The method of teaching LD students should be modified to suit their needs.
5. Care should be taken to see that they do not develop any inferiority complexes.
6. The provisions granted in this circular should be granted to all students at their class level once the student produces the necessary certificate of the competent authority mentioned in the State Board Circular.

Any difficulties / doubts regarding this subject will be discussed and sorted out in the office by the Deputy Director of Education every Monday at 4 p.m.

This information is to be given to all concerned.

Sd/

Deputy Director Education
Brinhanmumbai
http://www.disabilityindia.org/LDInstructions.html

MILESTONES

Excerpted below are just a few of many milestones a typically developing child reaches in the first year of life.

By 3 Months of Age

Motor Skills

1. Lift head when held at your shoulder.
2. Lift head and chest when lying on his stomach.
3. Turn head from side to side when lying on his stomach.
4. Follow a moving object or person with his eyes.
5. Grasp rattle when given to her.
6. Wiggle and kick with arms and legs.

Sensory and Thinking Skills

1. Turn head toward bright colors and lights.
2. Turn toward the sound of a human voice.
3. Recognize bottle or breast.
4. Respond to your shaking a rattle or bell.

Language and Social Skills

1. Make cooing, gurgling sounds.
2. Smile when smiled at.
3. Communicate hunger, fear, discomfort (through crying or facial expression).
4. Usually quietens down at the sound of a soothing voice or when held.

By 6 Months of Age

Motor Skills

1. Hold head steady when sitting with your help.
2. Reach for and grasp objects.
3. Play with his toes.
4. Help hold the bottle during feeding.
5. Explore by mouthing and banging objects.
6. Move toys from one hand to another.
7. Pull up to a sitting position on her own if you grasp her hands.
8. Sit with only a little support.
9. Roll over.
10. Bounce when held in a standing position.

Sensory and Thinking Skills

1. Open his mouth for the spoon.
2. Imitate familiar actions you perform.

Language and Social Skills

1. Babble, making almost sing-song sounds.
2. Know familiar faces.
3. Laugh and squeal with delight.
4. Scream if annoyed.
5. Smile at herself in a mirror.

By 12 Months of Age

Motor Skills

1. Drink from a cup with help.
2. Feed herself finger food like raisins.
3. Grasp small objects by using her thumb and index or forefinger.
4. Use his first finger to poke or point.

5. Put small blocks in and take them out of a container.
6. Knock two blocks together.
7. Sit well without support.
8. Crawl on hands and knees.
9. Pull himself to stand or take steps holding onto furniture.
10. Stand alone momentarily.
11. Walk with one hand held.

Sensory and Thinking Skills

1. Copy sounds and actions you make.
2. Respond to music with body motion.
3. Try to accomplish simple goals (seeing and then crawling to a toy).
4. Look for an object she watched fall out of sight (such as a spoon that falls under the table).

Language and Social Skills

1. Babble, but it sometimes 'sounds like' talking.
2. Say his first word.
3. Recognize family members' names.
4. Try to 'talk' with you.
5. Respond to another's distress by showing distress or crying.
6. Show affection to familiar adults.
7. Show apprehension about strangers.
8. Raise her arms when she wants to be picked up.
9. Understand simple commands.

ALTERNATE TERMS USED TO DESCRIBE LEARNING DISABILITY

lowing are terms used to identify learning disability. They
may not be correct. The list is presented here to make the
acquainted with the terms used.

ntion Deficit ·rder	• Slow Learner Dysfunction	• Minimal Brain
·ationally ·licapped	• Behavior Disorder	• Strephosymbolia
·ractivity ·rder	• Multi-sensory	• Word Blindness
·ological ·licap	• Neurologically Immature	• Dysphasic
·ss Syndrome	• Mildly Handicapped	• Dyscalculia
·ic Brain ·unction	• Language Disorder	• Puzzle Children
·ing Disability	• Diffuse Brain Damage	• Neorophrenia
·xia	• Dysgraphia	• Organicity
·nal Cerebral	• Hypo activity	• Maturation Lag
·opment ·ed	• Delayed learner	• Hyper kinesis
·iation Deficit ·logy	• Primary Reading Retardation	• Congenital Alexia
·tual Handicap	• Impulsive	

REFERENCES

1. Algozzine, B., Ruhl, K. and Ramsey, R. (1991) Behaviorally disordered? Assessment for identification and instruction. Reston, VA: The Council for Exceptional Children.

2. American Association for the Advancement of Science (2001) Dyslexia Study In *Science* Highlights The Impact Of English, French, And Italian Writing Systems. *Science Daily.*, http://www.sciencedaily.com **2009**

3. American Psychiatric Association. (2000). *Diagnostic and Statistical Manual of Mental Disorders* (4th ed., text rev.) (DSM-IV-TR). Washington, DC: American Psychiatric Association.

4. Ashar, S. (2005) Death wish. *Mid Day* (21.11.2005) Mumbai [online] http://ww1.midday.com/news/city/2005/november/123887.htm **2005**.

5. Ashcraft, M. (2002). Math anxiety: Personal, educational, and cognitive consequences. Current Directions in Psychological Science, 11(5), pp. 181-185.

6. Aster, M. and Shalev, R. (2007) Number development and developmental dyscalculia. *Developmental Medicine and Child Neurology*, 49, pp. 868-873.

7. Astin J. (1998) Why patients use alternative medicine: results of a national study. *Journal of the American Medical Association.* 1998;279(19):1548–1553

8. Atterbury, B. (1989). Being involved in mainstreaming decisions. *Music Educators Journal*, 75(6), 32–35.190

9. Berninger V, Smith D and O'Donnell L (2004) Research-Supported Assessment-Intervention Links for Reading and Writing

10. Brain briefing (2000) Brain Plasticity, Language Processing and Reading, *Society for Neuroscience* www.sfn.org **2008**

11. Bull, L, (2009) Survey of complementary and alternative therapies used by children with specific learning difficulties (dyslexia). *International Journal of Language & Communication Disorders*, e 44, 2 March 2009 , pages 224 - 235

12. Sharma, V (2004). Mind Publications: Adults too have learning disabilities. 2008 http://www.mindpub.com/art349.htm **2008**

13. Chivers, M.(2006) Dyslexia and Alternative Therapies Jessica Kingsley, London

14. Clark, C., Dyson, A., and Milward, A. (1995) Towards Inclusive Schools? London: David Fulton.

15. Colfer, J., Farrelly, M., Limerick, C., Grealy, T. and Smyth, F. (2000) A Place to learn: Inclusive Education for Children with Learning Disabilities. Discussion Document Psychological Society of Ireland Learning Disability Group. [online] http://www.psihq.ie/DOCUMENTS/A_PLACE_TO_LEARN. **2002**.

16. Colley, M. (2000) Living with Dyspraxia: A guide for Adults with Developmental Dyspraxia. Hitchin: Dyspraxia Foundation Adult Support Group

17. Cook, B. (2001) A Comparison of Teachers' Attitudes Toward Their Included Students with Mild and Severe Disabilities - Statistical Data Included. *Journal of Special Education* Winter.191

18. Cook, B. and Semmel, M. (1999) Peer acceptance of included students with disabilities as a function of severity of disability and classroom composition. *Journal of Special Education* 33: 50-61.

19. Cook, D., Skink, S. and Baynes D.(1994) Iron deficiency: the global perspective. *Adv Exp Med Biol* 1994; 356: pp. 219-228.

20. Cornwall, J. (1999) Pressure, stress and children's behavior. In David, T. (Ed.) *Young Children Learning*. Canterbury Christ Church University College, UK: Paul Chapman Educational Publishing.

21. Csikszentmihalyi, M. (1990) Flow: The psychology of optimum experience. New York: Harper-Collins.

22. Demonet J., Taylor, M., Chaix Y. (2004) Developmental dyslexia. *Lancet* 363: 1451 1460.

23. Deuel, R. (1995). Developmental Dysgraphia and Motor Skills Disorders. *Journal of Child Neurology*, Vol. 10, Supp.1. January 1995, pp. S6-S8.

24. Deuel, R.K. (1994). Developmental dysgraphia and motor skill disorders. *Journal of Child Neurology*, 10 (1), pp. 6-8.

25. DfES. (2001). *Guidance to support pupils with dyslexia and dyscalculia* (No. DfES 0512/2001). London: Department of Education

26. Dighe, A. and Kettles, G. (1996) Developmental dyspraxia - an overview. In G. Reid, (Ed.) Dimensions of dyslexia. V 2. *Literacy, Language and Learning*, pp. 231 – 263. Edinburgh: Moray House Publications.

27. Duchan, J. (2001). History of speech-pathology in America: Kurt Goldstein. http://www.ascu.buffalo.edu/~duchan/history_subpages/ **2007**

28. Edwards, J. (1994) The scars of dyslexia: eight case studies in emotional reactions. London: Cassell.

29. Elbaum, B. and Vaughn, S. (1999) Can school-based interventions enhance the self-concept of students with learning disabilities? [online] http://www.ncld.org/research/ncld_self_concept.cfm. **2002**.

30. Encyclopedia of Mental Disorders http://www.minddisorders.com/Py-Z/Reading-disorder.html 2008

31. Fiedorowicz. C. (2005) Neurobiological Basis of Learning Disabilities: An overview. The Learning Disabilities Association of Canada Research. http://www.ldactaac.ca/Research/neurobiological-e.asp **2008**

32. Fontana, D. (1995) Psychology for Teachers. New York: Macmillan.

33. Fredrickson, N. and T. Cline (2002) Special Needs: Inclusion and Diversity, a text book. Buckingham: Open University Press.

34. Goldman P. (2001) Herbal medicines today and the roots of modern pharmacology. *Annals of Internal Medicine* 2001;135(8):594-600.

35. Good, T. and Brophy, J. (1972) Behavioral Expression of Teacher Attitudes. *Journal of Educational Psychology* 63: 617-624.

37. Hallahan, D. and Cruickshank W. (1973) Psycho educational Foundation of Learning Disabilities. Englewood Cliffs, N.J.: Prentice-Hall.193 Brief History of Learning Disabilities

38. Hallahan, D. and Mercer, C. D. (2001). Learning disabilities, historical perceptions. Executive summary http://www.air.org;/ldsummit/**2008**

39. Hempenstall, K. (2006). What brain research can tell us about reading instruction. Learning Difficulties Australia Bulletin 38(1), 15-16.

40. Hinshelwood, J. (1917). Congenital word-blindness London: H. K. Lewis & Co. LTD.

41. IEDC (1986) Inclusive Education Scheme, Department of Education, India. http://www.education.nic.in/htmlweb/INCLUSIVE.htm **2005**.

42. *Individuals with Disabilities Education Act Amendments (IDEA) of 1997.* (1997). Public Law 105-17.

43. Johnson, B. (2005) Psychological comorbidity in children and adolescents with learning disorders. *Journal of Indian Association for Child and Adolescent Mental Health* 1 (1)

44. Johnson, D and Myklebust , H (1967) Learning Disabilities: Educational Principles and Practices. New York, Grune and Stratton, Inc

45. Jones, S. (1998). Accommodations and Modifications for Students with Handwriting Problems and/or Dysgraphia. Resource Room. http://www.resourceroom.net/readspell/dysgraphia.asp. **2005**

46. Kantrowitz, B, and Underwood, A, (1999) Tracking down the roots of dyslexia *Newsweek*, November 22, 1999

47. Karande S.(2008) Current challenges in managing specific learning disability in Indian children. J Postgrad Med 2008;54:75-7

48. Karande, S (2007) Medical Aspects of Specific Learning Disabilities (SpLD) http://www.tatalearningforum.com/TLD/presentations/Presentations/Session_2/Medical_Aspects/Dr_Sunil_Karande.ppt. **2009**

49. Karande, S and Kulkarni, M, (2005) Poor School Performance *Indian Journal of Pediatrics*, Nov.Volume 72

50. Karande, S., Satam, N., Kulkarni, M., Sholapurwala, R., Chitre, A., Shahi, N. (2007) Clinical and Psycho educational Profile of Children with Specific Learning Disability and Co-occurring Attention Deficit Hyperactivity Disorder. *Indian Journal of Medical Science* Vol. 61, No. 12

51. Karande,S., Mehta, V. and Kulkarni, M (2007) Impact of an education program on parental knowledge of specific learning disability *Indian J Med Sci* 2007;61:pp. 398-406

52. Karnath, P. (2001) Learning Disabilities in the Indian Context, The Nalanda Institute [online] http://www.nalandainstitute. org/aspfiles/learning.asp **2004.**

53. Kay, M. (2004). What is Dysgraphia? http://www.margaretkay. com/Dysgraphia.htm. **2008**

54. Kosc, L. (1974) Developmental Dyscalculia, *Journal of Learning Disabilities*, vol. 7, pp. 164-77, 1974.

55. Kulkarni M, Kalantre S, Upadhye S, Karande S, Ahuja S.(2001) Approach to learning disability. Indian J Pediatr 2001;68: pp. 539-46.

56. Kulkarni, M, and Karande, S. (2005) Specific Learning Disability: The Invisible Handicap *Indian Pediatrics*; 42: pp. 315-319

57. Lerner, J, (1997) Learning Disabilities: Theories, Diagnosis, and Teaching Strategies, Houghton Mifflin Co.

58. Maharashtra Government School Education Department G.R. No. SSC 1099/(151/99) HSE-2. November 2000. http://www. mah.nic.in/msec/; **2008,**

59. Maharashtra State Education, Research and Training Center, Pune Circular No. 96-97/3334. July 1996. Available at http://www.mah.nic.in/msec/; **2008,**

60. Medical News Today, 2009 Gene Associated With Language, Speech And Reading Disorders http://dx.doi.org/10.1007/s11689-009-9031-x **2009**

61. Miles, T and Varma, V. (Ed.) (1995) Dyslexia and Stress. London: Whurr Publications Ltd.

62. Miles, T. (1987) Understanding Dyslexia. Bath, UK: Bath Educational Publishers.

63. Morgan, W. (1896). A case of congenital word blindness. The British Medical Journal, 2, 1378.

64. Nation, K., Adams, J. W., Bowyer-Crane, C. A., and Snowling, M. J. (1999). Working memory deficits in poor comprehenders reflect underlying language impairments. *Journal of Experimental Child Psychology*, 73(2), 139–158.

65. National Information Center for Children and Youth with Disabilities (NICHCY) (2001). *General information about learning disabilities.* http://www.nichcy.org/pubs/factshe/fs17txt.htm. **2008**

66. NCCAM (2007) Publication No. D238 Reviewed October 2004 Updated March 2007

67. NCCAM (2007a) Publication No. D347Updated February 2007 http://nccam.nih.gov/health/whatiscam/overview.htm **2008**

68. NCCAM (2009) Publication No. D347 Updated February 2007 http://nccam.nih.gov/health/whatiscam/overview.htm **2008**

69. NCCAM (2009a) Publication No. D383 Created May 2007 Updated February 2009 http://nccam.nih.gov/health/children/**2008**

70. Orton, S. (1925). 'Word-blindness' in school children. Archives of Neurology and Psychiatry, 14, 581–615.

71. Ott, P. (1997) How to detect and manage dyslexia: a reference and resource manual Oxford: Heinemann.

72. PWD Act (1995) [online] http://www.disabilityindia.org/pwdacts.cfm **2003**.

73. Ramaa, S. (2000) Two Decades of Research on Learning Disabilities in India. *Dyslexia* (6): pp. 268-283.

74. Richards, R. (2002). When Writing's A Problem: Understanding Dysgraphia. Retrieved in Nov 2008 from http://www.dyslexia-ca.org/dysgraphia.htm. **2008**

75. Riddick, B. (1996) Living with dyslexia: The social and emotional consequences of specific learning difficulties. London: Routledge

76. Rourke, B. (1993). Arithmetic disabilities, specific and otherwise: A neuropsychological perspective. *Journal of Learning Disabilities*, 26(4), pp. 214-226.

77. Rutter, M. (1985) Resilience in the face of adversity. Protective factors and resistance to psychiatric disorder. *British Journal of Psychiatry* 147: pp. 598-611.

78. Saviour, P, and Ramachandra, N (2006) Biological basis of dyslexia: A maturing perspective *Current Science* vol 90 no 2 (25.1.2006)

79. Schuster, D. H and Vincent, L. (1980). Teaching math and reading with suggestion and music. *Academic Therapy,* 16, 69–72.

80. Science Daily (2008) Unraveling 'Math Dyslexia' *Science Daily* (Sep. 26, 2008) http://www.sciencedaily.com/releases/2008/09/080924151007.htm197 **2008**

81. Segelken, R. (2006). Further adventures of the incredible plastic brain. *Human Ecology*, 34(2), 16-19, http://www.human.cornell.edu/che/Outreach/upload/Further%20Adventures%20of%20the%20Incredible%20Plastic%20Brain.pdf **2008**

82. Shalev R,. Manor, O., Kerem, B., Ayali, M., Badichi, N., Friedlander, Y., and Gross-Tsur, V. (2001) Developmental dyscalculia is a familial learning disability *Journal of Learning Disabilities* vol. 34, pp. 59-65

83. Shalev, R (2004) Developmental Dyscalculia, *Journal of Child Neurology*, Vol. 19, No. 10, pp. 765-771

84. Shalev, R. and Gross-Tsur, V. (2001). Developmental dyscalculia. Review article. *Pediatric Neurology*, 24, 337–342.,

85. Shalev, R., and von Aster, M. G. (2008). Identification, classification, and prevalence of developmental dyscalculia. *Encyclopedia of Language and Literacy Development* (pp. 1-9). London, ON: Canadian Language and Literacy Research Network. http://www.literacyencyclopedia.ca/pdfs/topic.php?topId=253 **2008**

86. Shapiro K, and Gallico, P (1993) Learning disabilities Pediatric Clinic North Am; pp. 40: 491-505.

87. Sharma, M. (1990) Dyslexia, Dyscalculia, and some Remedial Perspectives for Mathematics Learning Problems *Math Notebook* Volume 8, No. 7-10 Framingham, MA: The Center for Teaching/Learning of Mathematics.

88. Sharma, Mahesh. 1990. "Dyslexia, Dyscalculia, and some Remedial Perspectives for Mathematics Learning Problems." *Math Notebook*. Volume 8, No. 7-10. (Sept. – Dec.) Framingham, MA: The Center for Teaching/Learning of Mathematics.

89. Sharma, R. (2003) Examination Stress claims one more casualty. Mid Day (2.2.2003) Mumbai.

90. Silberman, M. (1971) Teachers' attitudes and actions toward their students. In M. Silberman (Ed.) The *Experience of Schooling*, New York: Holt, Rinehart and Winston.

91. Society for Neuroscience Brain Plasticity, Language Processing and Reading Brain Briefing July 2005 www.sfn.org

92. Spinney, L(2009) Why some people can't put two and two together, *New Scientist* Magazine issue 2692 http://www.newscientist.com/article/mg20126921.700-why-some-people-cant-put-two-and-two-together.html?full=true **2009**

93. The British Dyslexia Association 9 (2009) http://www.bdadyslexia.org.uk/dyscalculia.html **2009**

94. The International Dyslexia Association Fact sheet (2008) Website: http://www.interdys.org **2009**

95. The Salamanca Statement (1994) The Salamanca Statement and Framework for Action on Special Needs Education. World Conference on Special Needs Education, Salamanca, Spain, UNESCO.[online] http://www.unesco.org/education/pdf/SALAMA_E.PDF. **2004**.

96. Nagarathna,(undated)http://www.healthandyoga.com/HTML/news/therapy/rtherapy73.asp **2008**

97. This article is published online courtesy www.vyasa.org and Arogyadhama http://www.healthandyoga.com/HTML/news/therapy/rtherapy73.asp

98. University of Western Ontario (2008) Unraveling 'Math Dyslexia' *Science Daily* http://www.sciencedaily.com/releases/2008/09/080924151007.htm **2008**

99. Vernetti, C., and Jacobs, J. (1972). Effects of music used to mask noise in learning disability classes. *Journal of Learning Disabilities*, 5, 533–537.

100. Wang, M., Reynolds, M. and Walberg, H. (1988) Integrating the children of the second system. *Phi Delta Kappa* 70: 248-251.

101. World Health Organization. (1996). Multiaxial classification of child and adolescent psychiatric disorders. Cambridge: Cambridge University Press. Adler,B (2001) What is dyscalculia? www.dyscalculiainfo.org **2007**

102. Yoshimoto, R. (2000) Celebrating Strengths and Talents of Dyslexic Children: An Educational Model. Perspectives, The International *Dyslexia Association* 26(2).

WORKSHEETS AND GAMES

Worksheets are a very important part of teaching. They provide students with means to practice a concept or skill they have already learnt in school. Some text books include practice exercises. However, these exercises are usually limited. For example, Maths is not a subject one learns by reading the problems and solutions. Children have to practice with multi-step problems. Continued practice is an effective approach to success with math. It is true for all students and especially true for a child with learning disability. English grammar worksheets help learners practice english grammar that they have learned in class.

In this book I am providing a few examples of worksheets. Furthermore, there are unlimited source of worksheets available on the internet for both students and teachers.

I am also including few simple games and exercises to ameliorate problems in gross and fine motor movement. While playing games as one has to follow the rules of the game similarly playing with one or more persons also enhances communication skills, decision making, planning and organization of thoughts, following instructions to name a few skills. Games and worksheets are always enjoyable activities. When children enjoy whatever they are doing, they are going through what Csikszentmihalyi (1990) calls a 'flow experience'. A flow experience is an experiential state that distinguishes an enjoyable moment from the rest of life. Research in education suggests that children learn more effectively when they are relaxed and enjoying themselves.

WORKSHEET 1

Exercises to Develop Gross Motor Skills

Gross motor skills include: balance–the ability to maintain equilibrium, body awareness–for improved posture and control, crossing of the mid-line, laterality, major muscle co-ordination and spatial orientation.

The following are suggestions of activities you can do with your child to develop gross motor skills. However, some children may need a much more specific program of activities. Occupational therapists and physiotherapists will need to assess the children's needs and advice on particular gross motor activities to address each child's specific difficulties. One should try and adapt the following activities according to ones child's proficiency.

• Play with a large ball. Encourage your child to kick the ball, using one foot and then the other. Then throw and catch it too

• Encourage your child to ride a bike, push bike or pedal bike with or without side-wheels, according to your child's ability

• Play 'Simon says - do this.' Say those words and do an action that your child must copy. When you say 'Simon says do that' she must NOT do the action

• To teach your child spatial relations. Ask her to stand in front of a chair, behind a chair, next to the chair, on top of the chair and crouch under the chair

• To develop her sense of laterality, let your child kneel on the floor, then instruct her in turn to lift her left hand, lift her right leg etc.

- Tell your child that she must be your shadow and mimic all your actions as you walk about and perform them.

- Learn action songs and perform the actions as you sing them

- Ask your child to imitate the movement of different animals: creep like a snake, waddle like a duck, hop like a rabbit etc. Crawling, hopping, etc. around the obstacles.

- Encourage her to balance first on one leg, then on the other for as long as possible.

- Skipping activities–individual and group skipping games (for example, 'Salt, mustard, vinegar, pepper')

- Sideways movements–jumping, walking, etc.

- Jumping over blocks–cardboard blocks covered with white paper

- Balancing activities–using a range of both small and large piece of equipment like a bench, a row of chairs, beam, plank, a line of tape and even a thick line painted on the floor teach them to balance. The child is expected to walk on the piece of equipment balancing herself. Bean bag movement is pretending to walk along a line of tape with a beanbag on her head

- Ask your child to imitate the movement of different animals: slither like a snake, waddle like a duck, hop like a rabbit, to gallop like a horse. Try Penguin waddle walking. (keep a small ball between knees and try to walk)

- Alphabet Body Contortion – form alphabets with your body. Get your child to copy. Practice spelling by forming the letters of the words with his/her body

Some Activities That Can be Carried out in School or with a Small Number of Children.

- Dodgems– Ask the children to run around in different directions, making sure that they do not bump into each other. They need to dodge out of the way of each other. You can make this game more difficult by calling out 'Change' so that they have to change direction.

- Stautes– Give each child a number, then ask them all to run around in different directions. If their number is called they have to stand still like a statue until the next number is called when they can move again.

- Stepping stones– Using small hoops as stepping stones, ask the children to 'cross the water' by jumping from one to the other without falling into the 'water'. Alternatively draw circles with chalk as steeping stones.

- Hopscotch

- Ball games– a range of games involving rolling, kicking, throwing and catching

- Batting activities – a range of games involving the use of bats, cricket stumps, sticks or racquets. These could be:

  o   Dribbling a ball around objects using a hockey stick

  o   Timing how long the children can keep a ball in the air by batting it

  o   Putting a ball into a specific position, using a hockey stick

  o   Paired games as in table tennis, racquet ball and short tennis

  o   Team games as in cricket and hockey

- Hula hoop musical chairs – Use several colors of hoops and lay them on the floor; play music; then dance around outside of the hoops. Call out 3 or 4 colors and the children have to stand in the hoop of the colors called out when the music is turned off.

- Jumping over the river – Use a blanket; start with it being narrow and the children should jump over it with two feet; gradually make it wider and they should try to jump over with out falling into the 'water'

WORKSHEET 2

Exercises to Develop Fine Motor Skills

- Pick up and sort objects such as blocks, coins, beans of different sizes like peanuts, chickpeas, broad beans , macaroni, marbles, pins, buttons, straws, nails, popcorn and place them into containers of with openings of varying sizes (i.e. like empty yogurt cartons, cups, mugs, bottles or jars)

- Stack objects like blocks, cards, books

- Pickup beans, seeds-like mustard seeds and nuts and with a spoon and transfer them from one container to another maintaining a proper grasp (the same as their pencil grasp)

- Play with plasticine or make silly putty: Pour one part liquid starch into two parts glue, a little at a time, and mix. Add more starch if needed (if the mixture is sticky). Cover and refrigerate it overnight.

- Make beads, small balls and different shapes; use different materials like plasticine, clay, dough and paper to make the beads. To make paper beads roll small strips of paper between fore-finger and thumb.

- Run a threaded needle through a cloth. Also take a large card punch holes into it and run wool or thread and needle through the holes.

- Cut straight and curved lines/shapes drawn on paper, or cloth with scissors.

- Type

- Crumple paper into a small ball and then flick it with the finger

- Shuffle cards, deal cards one by one, turn cards over

- Roll a pencil between thumb and fingers without dropping it.

- Knead dough

- Stick small objects into play dough for the child to pull out

- Wind thread on a spool evenly

- Put rubber bands around various size containers and objects

- Use tweezers to pick up small objects like cornflakes, thermo balls

- Move spoonfuls of small objects from one bowl to another

- Pre-Math skills: sort the items (beads in one bowl, buttons in another, beans in another) into a number of bowls/ or empty yoghurt cartons. Also sort the items by color

- Tie a box with string or ribbon

- Dial a telephone

- Color using the flat side of a crayon. Put paper over leaves, coins, stencils, and other objects so that the child gets sensory feedback as he colors.

- Spooning: Take two small bowls, one filled with dry rice. Practice fine motor skills by spooning rice from one bowl to the other

- Using eye droppers to pick up colored water for color mixing or to make artistic designs on paper

- Rolling small balls out of tissue paper, then gluing the balls onto construction paper to form pictures or designs

- Turning over cards, coins, checkers, or buttons, without bringing them to the edge of the table

- Have the child trace over your line drawing from left to right, or from top to bottom. Trace each figure at least 10 times then have the child draw the figure next to your model several times

- Play by connecting the dots; again, make sure the child's strokes connect dots from left to right, and from top to bottom

- Play throw and catch with a ball. Start with a large ball and work towards a smaller ball.

WORKSHEET 3

Some Games to Play

To teach colors

Play these games at home or classroom. Name the four corners of the room red, blue, yellow and green. Call out red, blue, yellow and green and the children have to run to the correct corner. Who so ever is left considered to be out.

Hide various objects (red, blue, yellow, green to start with) and ask children to find something red, blue, yellow and green. When they have all found an object, ask the children to form a circle and ask them in turn to say what color their object is. Then get all the children to pass their object to the child on their left. They should all have a different object and hopefully a different color. Repeat two or three times. Alternatively you can ask all of the children who have something 'red' to hold up their objects. *(Tip: do not use balls as they usually end up being thrown around.)*

Memory game

Place some different colored objects on a tray (start with a small number like six). Ask one of the children to close their eyes while you take away one of the objects. The child then has to say the color of the object which has been taken away.

Place different objects on a tray. Ask one child to close his eyes. Take away one object then ask him to name the object.

Play 'I went to the market and I bought..'

Quick puzzle

Take an empty cereal box cut the front part from it. Then cut it into pieces to form a puzzle. And then mix up the shapes. Put together like jigsaw puzzle.

Fine motor movement

Make salt dough toys and shapes.

Salt dough: 600 grams plain flour, 600 grams salt (600 grams = about 2 2/3 cups), 2 tablespoons oil, approximately 450 ml water (450 ml = about 2 cups), food coloring. Mix the flour, salt, oil, and food coloring and add the water a little at a time. Knead thoroughly. The children can create anything they like with this dough which can either air dry or be baked in a moderately hot oven.

Card games

All children enjoy card games. Most card games develop skills that facilitate learning in Maths like memory and concentration skills. Uno is a wonderful game to help children in development; this game teaches numbers, letters and matching. Children can practice counting back and forth, sequencing and ordering, additionally they have to learn to follow rules, planning and organizing their thoughts. Moreover, handling cards supports fine motor activity. The following are some more examples.

To teach number recognition, play 'Go Fish' and 'Sequence'. Sequence also teaches sequencing.

Go fish

The goal is to make as many matches as possible. The dealer passes out 5 cards to each player. The remaining cards are placed in the centre of the table and are used as the draw pile. Select a player to begin. The player whose turn it is selects a card from his hand and then chooses one of the players to ask if he/she has a card that matches that number. For example, the player looks at their hand and sees a 6. That player asks the other player, 'Do you have a 6?' If the player who received the question has the card, the card is given to the player who asked for it. The asking player takes another turn. The turns continue until the player does not receive a card from another player and has to 'go fish'. If the player who received the question does not have the card, that player tells the asking player to 'go fish'. The player then draws a card from the draw pile and their turn is completed. Play continues until all the cards have been matched. The player with the most matches wins the game.

Sequence

Best played with 4–5 children who are seven years and above; however, it is possible to play with as few as 2. Played with a standard deck of cards.

In this game, cards are ranked in numerical order (2, 3, 4, 5, 6, 7, 8, 9, 10, Knave, Queen, King, Ace). Cards of the same suit make up a sequence.

To start, the whole deck is dealt clockwise around the group, all dealt cards are kept face-down. It does not matter if the dealing is unequal.

The player to the left of the dealer places his lowest card with the face up on the table. Then, the player who has the next card (or cards) in the sequence plays it. The game continues until the entire sequence is complete, from 2 to Ace. Then, the next sequence is begun by whoever played the last card. The winner is the player who is the first to get rid of all his cards.

Dice games

Dice games are educational. They support counting skill and number recognition in little children, and quick mental addition in older children. Moreover, like card games they are also excellent at reinforcing the concept of following rules, taking turns, scoring (both mental and on paper), winning and losing patience.

Better this

(Teaches number recognition and understanding the value of the number)

Roll the dice and put them in order to make the highest number possible. If you roll a 2 and an 6, for example, your best answer would be 62. Using 3 dice, a roll of 1, 6 and 5 should give you 651, and so on. Write down your answer, pass the dice, and challenge the next player to 'Better This'

Keep your score

(Dice can be used to learn additions and multiplications.)

Roll the dice and note the number on the top. Roll another dice and again set aside. Note the count on the top. Roll the last dice, and add up your total. Write down your score. Play a number of rounds and then either total your points for the winner or simply count how many rounds were won by each player. The total can be achieved by using additions or multiplication.

Fun with writing (invisible ink)

(To teach neatness and consistency in accurately copying letters and words)

Ingredients

- White sheet of paper
- Lemon juice
- Cotton Buds
- Lamp

Writing secret messages

1. Dip the cotton-bud into the juice and smear the juice on the paper. Write your message on the paper.

2. Let the paper dry completely.

3. Have a parent remove the lamp.

4. Carefully place the paper over the hot light bulb (not too close!!!) and watch your message magically appear.

WORKSHEET 4

Reading

General Vocabulary Skills

Game to Develop Awareness

Make games out of sounds. You can play sound games almost anywhere: at dinner, in the car, while walking. Word play with sounds is a good way to develop phonemic awareness.

*   Rhyming Sounds: What words rhyme with can? For instance, pan rhymes with can.

*   Beginning Sounds: How many words can you make that start with the b sound?

*   Ending Sounds: How many words can you make that end with the 'sh' sound?

*   Rhyming Beginning Sounds: What word rhymes with rat but starts with the c sound?

*   Dropping Sounds: What happens when you drop the 'r' sound off of 'rat'?

*   Common Sounds: What sound do all of these words have in common: bat, big, ball, beg?

*   Blending Sounds: What word is made of these sounds: d and o and g?

Consonants produce sounds that are more consistent and easier to identify than vowels. Therefore, they make a good starting point for learning to read.

Initially, work should be done on identifying beginning consonant sounds (eg: t-t-t tub).

After that, activities can focus on identifying final consonant sounds (eg: cat ends with the t-t-t sound)

Viewing the word in the context of a picture will help reinforce this skill. For example, a picture of a dog with the word DOG underneath. The ability to sound out the D and G letters will help the child identify that the word is DOG, not puppy or Terrier)

WORKSHEET 5

Letter Recognition

Color the given alphabets according to the instruction given.

A - Pink   B - Yellow

C - Green   D - Blue

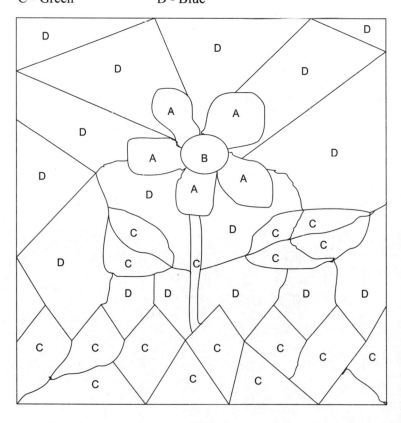

WORKSHEET 6

Coloring the B Objects

Color the objects begining with 'B'

WORKSHEET 7

The M Words

Read the word and circle the ones beginning with 'M'

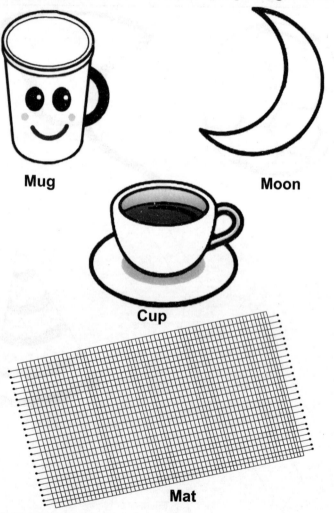

Mug

Moon

Cup

Mat

WORKSHEET 8

Rhyming Words

Write three words that rhyme with the words below

hat	ring		
1	1		
2	2		
3	3		
bed	rig		
1	1		
2	2		
3	3		
sad	pan		
1	1		
2	2		
3	3		
bear	car		
1	1		
2	2		
3	3		

WORKSHEET 9

Fill in the missing Letters

a e i l r o e a l e e t a r u g l l r i

N_ture	L_af
Plan_s	G_een
Se_ds	Ro_t
Flow_rs	Oxy_en
F__uits	Po_len
Soi_	M_nera_s
W_ter	Fe_til_zer
S_n	V_get_bles

WORKSHEET 10

Homophones

Find one homophone for each of the words given below

allowed	ball	base	beach	boy
check	days	die	due	faint
fur	great	in	key	lane
leek	war	waste	might	week
packed	pale	place	rain	read
profit	seen	road	sight	

WORKSHEET 11

Homophones

Write the Homophones for the given words.

plane	
see	
there	
which	
where	
be	
four	
no	
so	
knew	
flour	

WORKSHEET 12

Homophones

Choose the correct homophone and complete the sentences.

1. Illa could not wait to (meet/meat) her friend.

2. Lion ate the (meet/meat).

3. Raj (missed/mist) the train.

4. There is (mist/missed) on the window

5. The dog got his (tale/tail) caught.

6. Hema had to (wait/weight) for the bus.

7. Please (pour/poor/paw) the milk.

8. The beggar had no money as he was (pour/poor/paw).

9. There is a thorn in the cat's (pour/poor/paw).

WORKSHEET 13

Use of Wear, Where, Were

- **Wear** means to cover the body with clothes.

- **Where** means in what place or to what place or from what place.

- **Were** is used in all other cases.

Fill in the blanks with wear, were and where

1. I _____ warm clothes in Winter.

2. I do not know _____ Hema lives.

3. We _____ at the park yesterday.

4. _____ are you going this afternoon?

5. She had to _____ a ribbon in her hair.

6. When we _____ at the park we played.

7. People _____ sandals in summer.

8. _____ Uvi and Rhea at school?

9. _____ did the cat come from?

10. _____ can she be?

11. How many girls _____ with you?

12. _____ you at home yesterday?

13. This is the house _____ he lives.

14. _____ a blue ribbon today.

WORKSHEET 14

Scrabble Scramble

Another way to practice spelling words is to use the tile letters from a scrabble game. You can hand the letters that make up a word to your child and ask him/her to put them together. Or you can ask your child to pick them out without any help. Finally, you can play a game of scrabble using your child's spelled words..

WORKSHEET 15

Improving Reading Comprehension

- Choose a story at your child's reading level

- Read the story with your child

- Tell your child that you are going to read the story together again. This time, both you and the child will think about what the individuals/ creatures see, smell, hear, touch, and taste in the story

- As you read, be attentive to the descriptive words that describe what the individuals/ creatures experiences. Take a small break to talk about those sense experiences with your child

- Help your child write brief notes on the worksheet. If your child cannot write them independently, provide assistance

- Practice this activity occasionally, and keep the experience light and game-like

Over the time, your child will begin to notice more detail in stories and may even begin using more detail in her own writing

WORKSHEET 16

Count and color

Color Six apples red, Two apples pink, Four apples green

WORKSHEET 17

The Odd One

Circle the shape in each group that is different.

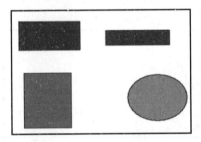 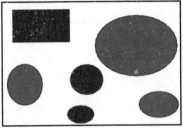

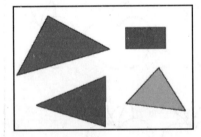 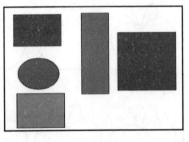

WORKSHEET 18

Count and Color

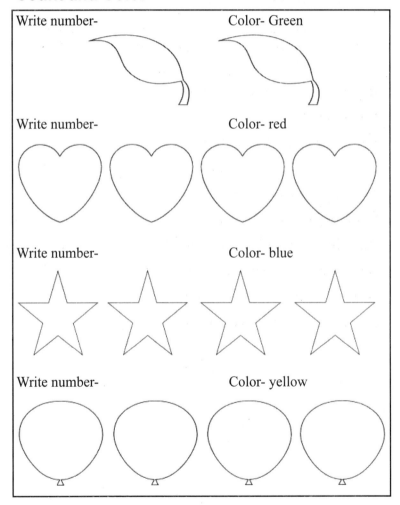

Write number-   Color- Green

Write number-   Color- red

Write number-   Color- blue

Write number-   Color- yellow

WORKSHEET 19

Before Maths

Let the child count the objects and either of you can write the number in the space provided. Have fun with this exercise.

How many chairs are in your house? _____

How many chairs are there at the dining table? _____

How many people live with you? _____

How many windows are there? _____

How many doors are there? _____

How many tigers live in your house? _____

How many pair of shoes do you have? _____

How many pair of shoes are there in the house? _____

How many coins are there in this purse? _____

How many spoons are there on the table? _____

WORKSHEET 20

Understanding 1 less (for 2 players)

Roll two dices.

Cover up the number which is 1 less than that number.

1	2	3	6	7	8
9	10	11	12	1	12
4	5	7	1	9	2
2	6	3	11	5	7
8	12	3	4	8	10
9	11	12	6	1	0
12	9	7	8	3	10

WORKSHEET 21

Understanding 1 more (for 2 players)

Roll two dices.

Cover up the number which is 1 more than that number.

3	4	5	6	7	8
9	10	11	12	1	12
10	6	7	1	9	2
2	6	3	11	5	7
8	12	3	4	8	10
9	11	12	6	1	0
12	9	7	8	3	10

WORKSHEET 22

Counting Forwards And Backwards

Forwards

1		3		5	
7	8		10		12
15		17		19	
19			22		24
18		20	21		23
31		33		35	
37		39		41	

Backwards

5		3		1	
7		5	4		2
10		8		6	
12		10	9		7
15		13			10
20		18		16	
22		20		18	

WORKSHEET 23

Which Number Is Bigger?

Look at the number in the square. Circle the bigger number. Then write the number 10 times.

3, 5, 7	_____
1, 2, 3	_____
4, 6, 8	_____
9, 5, 4	_____
3, 4, 5	_____

WORKSHEET 24

Puzzling Shapes

Look at the picture below how many rectangles can you see?

Write down the number_____

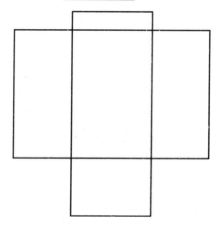

Look at the picture below how many triangles can you see?

Write down the number_____

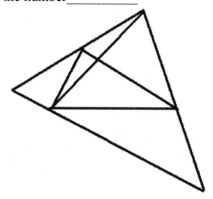

WORKSHEET 25

Addition Facts Table

Look at the table carefully. It teaches you how to add

+	1	2	3	4	5	6	7	8	9	10
1	2	3	4	5	6	7	8	9	10	11
2	3	4	5	6	7	8	9	10	11	12
3	4	5	6	7	8	9	10	11	12	13
4	5	6	7	8	9	10	11	12	13	14
5	6	7	8	9	10	11	12	13	14	15
6	7	8	9	10	11	12	13	14	15	16
7	8	9	10	11	12	13	14	15	16	17
8	9	10	11	12	13	14	15	16	17	18
9	10	11	12	13	14	15	16	17	18	19
10	11	12	13	14	15	16	17	18	19	20

Learn addition facts one at a time.

+	1	2	3	4	5	6	7	8	9	10
1	2	3	4	5	6	7	8	9	10	11
2	3	4	5	6	7	8	9	10	11	12
3	4	5	6	7	8	9	10	11	12	13
4	5	6	7	8	9	10	11	12	13	14
5	6	7	8	9	10	11	12	13	14	15
6	7	8	9	10	11	12	13	14	15	16
7	8	9	10	11	12	13	14	15	16	17
8	9	10	11	12	13	14	15	16	17	18
9	10	11	12	13	14	15	16	17	18	19
10	11	12	13	14	15	16	17	18	19	20

WORKSHEET 26

Blank Addition Facts Table

Add the numbers on the top line (horizontal) with the first (vertical) line and see if you get the correct answer or not

+	1	2	3	4	5	6	7	8	9	10
1										
2										
3										
4										
5										
6										
7										
8										
9										
10										

Complete the following table

+	3	2	8	6	1	5	9	4	10	7
8	11	10	16	14	9					
3	6									
4	7									
10	13									
7										
6										
9										
1										
5										
2										

RESOURCES FOR WORKSHEETS

www.senteacher.org

www.readingtarget.com/

http://www.yourdictionary.com/grammar-rules/free-spelling-printables.html

http://www.handwritingworksheets.com/

http://www.softschools.com/

http://www.sitesforparents.com/cgi-bin/autorank/search.cgi?key=works

http://www.sitesforteachers.com/index2.html

http://www.zozanga.com/

http://www.akidsheart.com/

http://www.akidsheart.com/color.htm

http://www.teach-nology.com/worksheets/

http://www.ezschool.com/worksheets/

http://www.enchantedlearning.com/

http://school.discovery.com/.

http://www.schoolexpress.com/

http://www.abcteach.com/

http://www.kidsdomain.com/

http://faculty.washington.edu/chudler/wo...

http://choreworksheetsforkids.com/

http://www.beginningreading.com/